Coaching
Skills Training Course

Business and life coaching techniques for improving performance using NLP and goal setting

Downloadable templates ready to use

Kathryn Critchley

Coaching Skills Training Course

Business and life coaching techniques for improving performance using NLP and goal setting. Your toolkit to coaching yourself and others with exercises and scripts. Free downloadable templates, ready to use. (Skills Training Course)

Published by: Universe of Learning Ltd, reg number 6485477, Lancashire, UK
www.UoLearn.com, support@UoLearn.com

ISBN 978-1-84937-019-6

Other editions:
ebook pdf format 978-1-84937-013-4
ebook epub format 978-1-84937-014-1
UK spelling version 978-1-84937-001-1

Photographs by various artists, © www.fotolia.com
Cover photo © nyul, www.fotolia.com

Dedication

I dedicate this book to my parents, Margaret and James Critchley

Who are the two most precious people on this earth to me. They have always encouraged me, given me great confidence in myself, shown me a better path than they were blessed with, picked me up, dusted me down and pointed me in the right direction many, many times and loved me with the deepest love. Thank you for always being there and for helping to create the person I have become. I love you both with all my heart and will be eternally grateful for all you have done for me.

I thank my friends and family, especially my brother Drew, Uncle Chris, Mark, Sam, Liz, Simon and Sal who have encouraged and loved me, been patient with me and supported me during good times and bad.

Also to Ollie who has been my faithful pal for the past 12 years, he's like my little guardian angel and is the best and most faithful friend anyone could be blessed with.

A heartfelt thanks to you all.

Special thanks to:
Jane Howitt for being a part of the initial process and her great encouragement.
Margaret Greenhall for her efforts, ideas and inspiration.
Sally Hayes and Dave Smith for their wonderful photographs.

About the author
Kathryn Critchley,
Realife Ltd

Kathryn is a highly skilled and experienced trainer, coach and therapist.

With over 14 years experience of high-pressure sales and management roles in the telecoms industry with organizations such as BT and Orange, Kathryn understands the dynamics of team-building, change management, employee motivation and organizational productivity.

She has provided training, coaching or therapy for organizations such as BT, Orange, Peugeot, Cisco Systems, IBM, British Gas, Victim Support and Witness Service, NHS and various councils, schools and universities.

Kathryn is passionate about helping people make positive changes and achieve their goals. She achieves remarkable results through seminars and workshops, as well as one to one interventions. Her website is www.realifeltd.co.uk

In this book she shares some of the knowledge and skills that have helped her to be a successful business and personal coach.

Contents

CONTENTS

Session number	Tool	Establish your starting point	Structure of a coaching session	Learning styles	Decision making	Processing information	Sensory learning	Perception of self	Perception of others	Behavioral types	Conflict resolution
1	Life areas assessment	x			x						
2	The 3 W's		x								
	Kolb's learning cycle			x						x	
	Learning styles			x	x	x				x	
	Sensory learning			x		x	x			x	
	Transactional analysis			x				x	x	x	
	Conscious perception					x		x	x	x	x
	Good coach?	x						x			
3	Match and mirror										
	Eye accessing			x			x			x	
	Questioning					x	x				
	Summarizing								x		
	Feedback								x		
4	Modeling				x		x	x	x		
	New behavior script				x		x	x	x		
	Anchoring script				x		x	x	x		
	Pattern breakers					x	x			x	
	Self coach exercise	x						x			
	Commitment Letter	x			x			x			
	Positivity letter							x			
	Relaxation						x				
	Chunking					x					x
4,5	Sun diagrams	x			x	x					
	Outcomes	x			x						
	Goal setting	x			x						
	STEPPA	x			x						
	TGROW	x			x						

Challenging perspectives	Self assessment	Building rapport	Assessing others	Questioning skills	Summarizing	Giving feedback	Receiving feedback	Listening skills	Changing beliefs	Changing strategies	Goal setting	Questionnaires	Scripts
X	X		X	X	X					X		X	
		X	X	X	X	X							
	X		X										
	X	X	X						X			X	
		X	X	X				X					
X	X		X						X				
X			X	X		X	X		X	X			
	X		X				X					X	
		X	X										
		X	X										
X			X	X									
X		X	X	X	X	X		X					
X			X			X				X			
X									X	X			
X									X	X			X
X									X	X			X
X				X		X			X	X			
X	X						X			X		X	
X	X								X	X			
X	X								X	X			
X										X			X
X		X	X	X	X			X					
X	X			X	X					X	X		
X	X									X	X	X	
X	X								X	X	X		
X	X								X	X	X		
X	X								X	X	X		

Introduction
Coaching skills training course

This book will help you to:

✓ Acquire new skills and strategies to self-coach and improve every area of your life

✓ Utilize coaching to improve your skills as a leader and manager, to help yourself and others reach ultimate peak performance

✓ Enhance your communication, language skills and confidence using NLP and various performance coaching methods

Course overview

We start this course by taking an in-depth look at what coaching is, when it would be used and what it involves, giving you an exact understanding of the process and its boundaries. With coaching, you are in control of your life and not the other way around.

Extra resources

If you visit the coaching section of the website www.UoLearn.com then you can find a free printable workbook with all the exercises from this book. You'll also find blank templates ready for you to download and use in your own time.

How to use this program

Welcome to the Coaching Skills Training Course. We have designed this workbook to be a tool-kit of the ultimate coaching skills. It is interactive and multi-functional in that you can learn to self-coach, coach others or both. The program starts by explaining the tools, strategies and practical exercises in each section followed by practical tips from the 'Coaching Corner' on how to apply the skills to assist others and 'Personal Reflection' explaining how to use the tools for maximum effect for yourself.

It is important that you work through the program in the correct order of sessions to ensure that you collect the skills as you go along, building up to larger exercises and full coaching sessions. We recommend learning to self-coach before attempting to practice on others, to gain a full understanding and empathy of the process.

Coaching is becoming more and more popular, as is therapy. Yet there are so many different kinds, and so many crossovers and similarities between the methods available, that the whole thing can get very confusing – where do you set your focus? Ultimately we all want what will work best for us, and if you're a manager seeking to enhance the skills of your team, you'll want what works best for them!

With that in mind, we've selected what we feel are the best strategies from various coaching styles including a few directive therapies. We've put them all together so that you can learn to help yourself (or self-coach), and develop the skills to help others.

Remember, this is not a program designed to make you into a coach – it is to give you coaching skills. The skills are for you to use for yourself or to add to your management and leadership skills to get the best out of your team and individuals.

Used correctly, coaching offers highly effective tools for positive change and focused direction in your life. It helps you find a way around any challenge, achieve more (including things you thought you could never do) and create a clear focused direction for your future.

Warning!

NLP and coaching are just two of many styles of coaching and development. If you have issues in your life where you need specific help or guidance DO NOT rely solely on the tools, techniques and advice in this program – get appropriate professional help. Remember that this course will also provide you with skills and tools to help others but you will not be qualified as a professional coach nor will you receive any formal qualification from this program. Be aware of your boundaries and seek help or refer people for professional help should they need it.

Disclaimer

Please read this carefully before you start the Coaching Skills Training Course.

The information in this Coaching Skills Course is for educational purposes only and is solely the opinion of the author. It is in no way a substitute for advice, support and guidance provided during a private session with a coach or medical professional, and is not intended to advise or suggest. Neither the publisher nor the author directly or indirectly dispense advice, nor do they prescribe any remedies or assume any responsibility for those who choose to treat and self-coach themselves or coach others.

Important cautions

The program's creators, producers and distributors cannot guarantee that this program is safe and proper for every individual. For that reason, this program is sold without warranties or guarantes of any kind.

Any liability, loss or damage in connection with any use of this program, including but not limited to any liability, loss or damage resulting from the advice and information given here, is expressly disclaimed.

Unique approach

Our course is different from most because it takes a dual approach to coaching. It looks at how to coach yourself but also covers how it would be appropriate to use those skills to help others.

It includes exercises for you to complete which you can then adapt if you want to use them with your team or in your department. You need to work through this program to ensure you fully understand the tools and strategies demonstrated and that you have a firm understanding of the coaching process – you cannot help others until you have helped yourself!

Based on various coaching and therapy techniques – including NLP (Neuro Linguistic Programming), Performance Coaching, Life Coaching, Modeling, CBT (Cognitive Behavioral Therapy) and TA (Transactional Analysis) – this course allows you to consider all the best strategies and solutions and make your own conclusions. You don't have to use them all – just choose which fit you best; that's why we give you a selection.

Although we use many different theories and strategies, we keep it simple, easy to understand and easy to apply.

Successful self-coaching

Learning about yourself, discovering your strengths and areas for improvement, having an open mind, being open to and accepting of change, being able to take (calculated) risks and being free to make mistakes (and learn from them) is the basis for good self-management. Identifying a starting point is essential. No matter how good or bad you think that starting point is it's something you can build from.

Remember: If just one human being has achieved something, then it can be done. And if nobody has achieved it yet, perhaps you can to be that one human.

Successful management

Once you've completed some self-analysis and learnt how to self-coach, you'll be equipped to help others.

Coaching is different from managing or leading – it's a specific technique that enhances management and leadership skills and qualities. It is directive, but it's not about giving direction – that's for the coachee to figure out for themselves. Your role is to assist, challenge, give clarity, and encourage options and opportunities. This helps the coachee build the confidence, motivation and independence to learn to self-coach and take responsibility for their continued long-term development.

This course is a little different, informal and lots of fun. All we ask is that you open your mind, take from it what is right for you, and enjoy!

Kathryn Critchley

Course objectives:

By the end of this course you will:

✓ Understand the role of coaching, its boundaries and how it can enhance your life.

✓ Understand how to self-coach and have a fixed action plan and goals for how to make the changes you desire – and be already making those changes!

✓ Have a range of coaching skills to use at work and at home.

✓ Be able to confidently support individuals and groups in developing and implementing strategies to achieve their objectives based around their roles.

✓ Have the skills and tools to walk you through the process – set strategies and scripts for you to use and adapt.

What are your objectives for this course?

What would you like to get from it?

What are you looking to change or develop?

List your objectives below.

Exercise: My objectives

Coaching corner

Starting coaching

3 things your coachee will need:

When you first start to work with a coachee you will need to establish what they wish to achieve. This is not something you can do for them or give them. They need to be clear about where they are now and where they want to go. I call this their point A (start) and point B (goal or end point). You can then go on to explore 'how' to get there which is the coaching part.

There are 3 essential things you will need from every coachee you work with to be able to conduct an effective coaching session.
1. They know what they want/need to achieve.
2. They want to achieve it.
3. They want to have coaching.

Even if a coachee does not know what they want from life, their start point could be, point A – I don't know what I want to do with my life. Point B – I want to know what I want to do with my life. The session will then be around exploring options and possibilities to narrow them down by eliminating areas which don't appeal until the coachee gets some clarity and direction. (Which may not be just in one session so don't put any pressure on yourself to have all the answers – it's the coachee who has the answers!)

Most coachees will have specific areas they wish to work on but it doesn't matter if they don't, as shown in the example discussed. The crucial thing is to ensure that they have the 3 essential things for all coaching sessions.

Personal reflection – The importance of your goals and establishing a starting point

At the end of this program we encourage you to choose one of the 3 goal setting models we have given you to set your own goals and objectives from 1 month up to the next 3-5 years. It is so important for you to have goals as they are something to aim at, a direction to go in, even if you decide further down the line to change, adapt or even discard them. It has been said that an unwritten goal is just a dream. Establishing your goals and putting a stake in the ground gives you a start and end point i.e. a point A and a point B. Coaching is all about finding out how to get from A to B and what the journey will entail along the way. Start to consider what you want from life, your career, relationships, finances and health, etc. If you do not know these then you will always be reactive to life rather than pro-active to taking control of your life and moving towards things/areas that you want to achieve.

The next session will help you to establish your start point A and by the end of this program you will have established your end point B and have many ways to consider how to achieve it/them.

Start now to think about what you want from your life.

Session 1

The Coaching Concept

"A single conversation with a wise person
is better than ten years of study."

Session 1

The coaching concept

Objectives for session 1:

When you've studied this session, you should be able to:

- ✓ Explain what coaching is, and how it can help improve performance

- ✓ Describe how NLP works and how it's an effective coaching tool

- ✓ List some of the changes you want to make through self-coaching

Tools in session 1:

- ✓ Life Areas Assessment – for your starting point

What are coaching and NLP?

Coaching

> "*Coaching is a process that enables learning and development to occur and thus performance to improve. To be successful, a coach requires knowledge and understanding of process as well as the variety of styles, skills and techniques that are appropriate to the context in which the coaching takes place.*"
> (Eric Parsloe, 1999)

Coaching can be used for many purposes, ranging from life coaching, career coaching, performance coaching through to sports coaching and health. Anything that a person wishes to achieve can be enhanced and progressed with the assistance of a great coach.

Coaching is future-focused and about effective change management. It involves setting goals, having a clear direction of future wants, needs and desires and discovering ways to achieve such goals

Professional coaching is an interactive process that helps individuals and organizations improve their performances and achieve extraordinary results. Professional coaches work with coachees in all areas including business, career, finances, health and relationships. As a result of professional coaching, coachees set better goals, take more action, make better decisions, and more fully use their natural strengths. (The Coaching Federation)

NLP

> Neuro linguistic programming (NLP) is a form of coaching in its own right and works in harmony with any directive coaching or therapy style. It's an excellent tool for making swift changes by understanding yourself, your thoughts and behavior patterns, even down to what words you choose and commonly use to 'program' yourself and others. Once you identify a pattern or belief you can then change it and put a set plan into practise.

"NLP studies what works in thinking, language and behavior. It's a way of coding and reproducing excellence, enabling you to consistently achieve the results you want, for yourself, for your business, and for your life." (Sue Knight, 2002)

It brings together three areas:

➢ Neuro refers to the workings of the mind and how we think.

➢ Linguistic refers to language patterns, how we use language and how we are influenced by it; these patterns can be both verbal and non-verbal.

➢ Programming refers to the way in which thoughts and language can be arranged into patterns of behavior and how these patterns can be changed.

You can use NLP for a variety of needs – breaking and redefining unwanted patterns of behavior, curing phobias and fears, assessing character and personality types, building confidence and esteem, 'state' management and creating and developing excellence in any field.

It's a brief and short-term active process with lasting results, which is why we've included many NLP models for you to try. Parts of this course such as anchoring, pattern breakers, eye accessing cues and some of the goal setting models are taken from NLP.

If you have an interest in NLP as a coaching tool there is a list of books for further reading in the reference and further reading section of this program.

During this program we focus mainly on performance coaching, integrating NLP and a few other excellent methods, showing you how to utilize these skills for yourself and for enhancing the skills of individuals and teams as an effective manager and leader.

Performance coaching
– the benefits

The benefits of performance coaching can be huge, achieving tremendous results in a much shorter time frame. Performance coaching in particular can help with:

✓ Improved performance and productivity

✓ Enhanced motivation

✓ Better quality of life and work/life balance

✓ Gaining and enhancing skills and knowledge

✓ Better use of people, skills and resources

✓ Improved relations between individuals and departments

✓ Encouraging more creative ideas

✓ Greater flexibility and adaptability

✓ Ability to embrace change

✓ Opportunities to acquire new and different skills

Coaching:

- ✓ Involves a structured process of coaching methods
- ✓ Provides a non-judgmental, open and honest environment
- ✓ Enhances learning through self-discovery rather than being told what to do.
- ✓ Offers the freedom to learn and grow without worry of failure or criticism
- ✓ Gives encouragement and motivation
- ✓ Provides confidentiality, trust and support

Coaching is effective for many situations but at work you'd focus on topics such as:

- ➢ Any form of organizational or individual role change
- ➢ Individual growth and development
- ➢ Improving skills and knowledge
- ➢ Improving productivity and performance
- ➢ New and existing team building and bonding
- ➢ Performance reviews or appraisals
- ➢ Recruiting new team members
- ➢ Introduction of new technology, services, systems and procedures
- ➢ New or existing projects
- ➢ Working with difficult individuals
- ➢ Managing conflict
- ➢ Working with individuals' personal issues affecting their work
- ➢ Promoting employees and new roles/role changes

Your starting point:

Exercise: Take a look at yourself.
What do **you** think of **you**?
What would you like to change, gain, eliminate or enhance?
(Think about your personal and work life – yourself,
knowledge and skills.)

....
....
....
....
....
....

How confident are you?
On a scale of 0 to 10, where 0 = lacking in confidence and
10 = massively confident:

0	1	2	3	4	5	6	7	8	9	10
☹	○	○	○	○	☺	○	○	○	○	☺

How happy are you?
On a scale of 0 to 10, where 0 = utterly miserable and
10 = ecstatically happy:

0	1	2	3	4	5	6	7	8	9	10
☹	○	○	○	○	☺	○	○	○	○	☺

Life Areas Assessment

Let's break this down into more specific areas, to identify some starting points for you to focus on throughout the program. Look at the categories below.

Rate how happy you are with each life area or issue, with 0 = desperately unhappy and 10 = extremely happy.

Don't think too deeply about it, just go with your first thought. If a particular item isn't right for you, just miss it out. For example, if you don't have children, then ignore the parenting section; or if you don't consider yourself religious or spiritual, then feel free to skip that section. It won't affect the results.

	0	1	2	3	4	5	6	7	8	9	10
Finances	☹	○	○	○	○	☺	○	○	○	○	☺
Career/job	☹	○	○	○	○	☺	○	○	○	○	☺
Mental health	☹	○	○	○	○	☺	○	○	○	○	☺
Physical health	☹	○	○	○	○	☺	○	○	○	○	☺
Friends	☹	○	○	○	○	☺	○	○	○	○	☺
Family	☹	○	○	○	○	☺	○	○	○	○	☺
Parenting	☹	○	○	○	○	☺	○	○	○	○	☺
Partner	☹	○	○	○	○	☺	○	○	○	○	☺
Personal dev.	☹	○	○	○	○	☺	○	○	○	○	☺
Fun, recreation	☹	○	○	○	○	☺	○	○	○	○	☺
Home	☹	○	○	○	○	☺	○	○	○	○	☺
Spirituality	☹	○	○	○	○	☺	○	○	○	○	☺

Your scores should give you an idea which areas need work.

It's important to note that you're not necessarily aiming for everything being 10. For some people a lower figure is sufficient and the numbers and their significance are relative to the individual anyway.

If your numbers differ wildly – some high figures along with some very low figures – that's indicative of a lack of balance in life. Your aim is to have a healthy balance which is then maintained, throughout all of the life areas.

So now you have identified which are the priority areas for you to address, you can focus your attention on these throughout the rest of the program. If there are no main issues for you to concentrate on, you can focus on maintaining the balance you've already achieved, but for most of us, there's always something we want to work on, gain or improve.

If you're using this program to help your team or department, you can get them to complete the Life Areas Assessment Tool or you can adapt it by adding specific areas or titles to match your context.

We've created a Health Assessment Tool to give you an example of how you can use the tool for any area, personal or work-related:

Health Assessment Tool

	0	1	2	3	4	5	6	7	8	9	10
Healthy eating	☹	○	○	○	○	☺	○	○	○	○	☺
Hydration	☹	○	○	○	○	☺	○	○	○	○	☺
Aerobic exercise	☹	○	○	○	○	☺	○	○	○	○	☺
Resistance exer.	☹	○	○	○	○	☺	○	○	○	○	☺
Fitness level	☹	○	○	○	○	☺	○	○	○	○	☺
Weight	☹	○	○	○	○	☺	○	○	○	○	☺
Sleep	☹	○	○	○	○	☺	○	○	○	○	☺
Energy levels	☹	○	○	○	○	☺	○	○	○	○	☺
General health	☹	○	○	○	○	☺	○	○	○	○	☺
Relaxation	☹	○	○	○	○	☺	○	○	○	○	☺

We'll be returning to your starting point later in the program to show you how to make the changes you desire. We'll need you to break each section down into more specific goals; for example, if you've chosen 'finances' as a priority area to address, what specifically do you need to address? Perhaps that is something you can start to think about now.

Coaching corner

The importance of self-coaching

If you are using this program with a view to coaching others it is essential that you work through each of these sessions and complete the exercises yourself, i.e. to self-coach before you consider coaching others. This will give you a thorough understanding of how to use the tools so that you can explain them to your coachee. It will also give you the understanding and empathy of what it feels like to complete them and how the results or process can affect how you feel too. You will then have a much greater understanding to enable you to be a more effective coach. You will need to engage with the activities in the book to find out how they work. You may also be surprised by some of your results, observations and realizations of yourself along the way, enabling you to grow and develop by applying positive changes.

Personal reflection –
Using the life areas assessment tool

Once you have completed the Life Areas Assessment you may be a little surprised by the results. If you are this is fine, it is just giving you more awareness of areas that you may wish to address. We generally focus on the lower scored areas but this is not always the case. If something has scored higher but is a priority area for you that you wish to address to get a higher score then this will be your starting point. I personally recommend that we all work on all of the areas shown in the list. Some people work too much yet neglect their health, others may spend too much time with friends and not enough in their relationship, others may have financial issues which affect their mental health (cause them stress or anxiety), most people have imbalances so if you have too this is very normal and okay. So you can relax and take action to make it how you would like it to be.

This is a simple tool, yet a very valuable one and one which should be used frequently to identify areas of change/improvement but also to monitor such change and improvement to ensure the best possible balance is achieved for you.

Session 2

The Coaching Process

"The greatest good you can do for another is not just to share your riches but to reveal to him his own."

Benjamin Disraeli

Session 2

The coaching process

Objectives for session 2:

After working through this chapter you should be able to:

✓ Describe the differences between coaching and therapy

✓ Explain the ground rules of coaching to a coachee

✓ Demonstrate a working outline of a coaching session

✓ Create a list of useful coaching tools and exercises

✓ Understand the different learning, behavioral and personality types

✓ Explain the coaching dos and don'ts

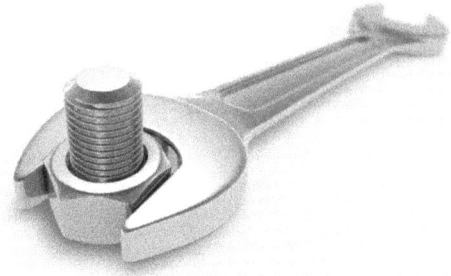

Tools in session 2:

- ✓ The 3 W's – to structure a basic coaching session
- ✓ Kolb's Learning Cycle – understanding how we learn
- ✓ Honey and Mumford Learning Styles – understanding how people want and process information plus make decisions differently
- ✓ Sensory Learning (NLP VAKOG model) – how people use the senses such as sight, sound and touch/feelings to understand plus process information
- ✓ Thomas Harris I'm OK, You're OK Transactional Analysis Model – used to understand how people see themselves and others
- ✓ Conscious Perception – used to help people to see things from different perspectives and also great for conflict resolution
- ✓ Will You Be A Good Coach questionnaire – self assessment of coaching skills and ability

Coaching requirements and their boundaries

Coaching unlocks a person's potential to maximize their performance.

> Coaching is about helping people to learn, rather than teaching them.
>
> It's about planning and action, feedback and reflection.
>
> It is goal-orientated and results-focused.

Differences between Coaching and Therapy

Psychotherapy and counseling usually focus on the past, feelings and emotions and the reasons why issues occurred. Coaching is focused on the future. It accepts that emotions and pain can exist from the past but focuses more on what to do about them in the now and the future, rather than looking back to resolve the past.

There is always an overlap, as some therapy has a more directive style similar to coaching so is more future-focused. There are also times when a coach will take a brief look at the past to gain some understanding of the kind of change required.

Coaching tends to focus on more short-term, quick change (generally just a few sessions or sometimes as little as one session is all that is required to create the desired lasting change) whereas therapy can be a much longer process, some psychotherapy can take place over several years.

Transformational process

Effective performance coaching can transform individuals and organizations. It unlocks people's potential helping them to discover their strengths and increase their performance. Working with a coach can help individuals and teams make changes faster and more effectively than they would on their own.

The coach facilitates the coachee's learning so they can find new ways of thinking about and understanding their role and objectives within the workplace.

The process helps them to discover new choices and encourages them to find a viable path to their goal, motivating them to succeed. The coach supports the achievement of the goal. The coachee is able to learn new and more positive ways of experiencing barriers to their objectives and find ways to overcome such obstacles.

Coaching style

Teaching or instructing someone is less effective in the long term than allowing them to experience and learn by themselves. The following graph (Robert Pike 1994) demonstrates that people learn best by a combination of being told, shown and their own experience, which is why coaching is one of the most effective ways of helping people to learn.

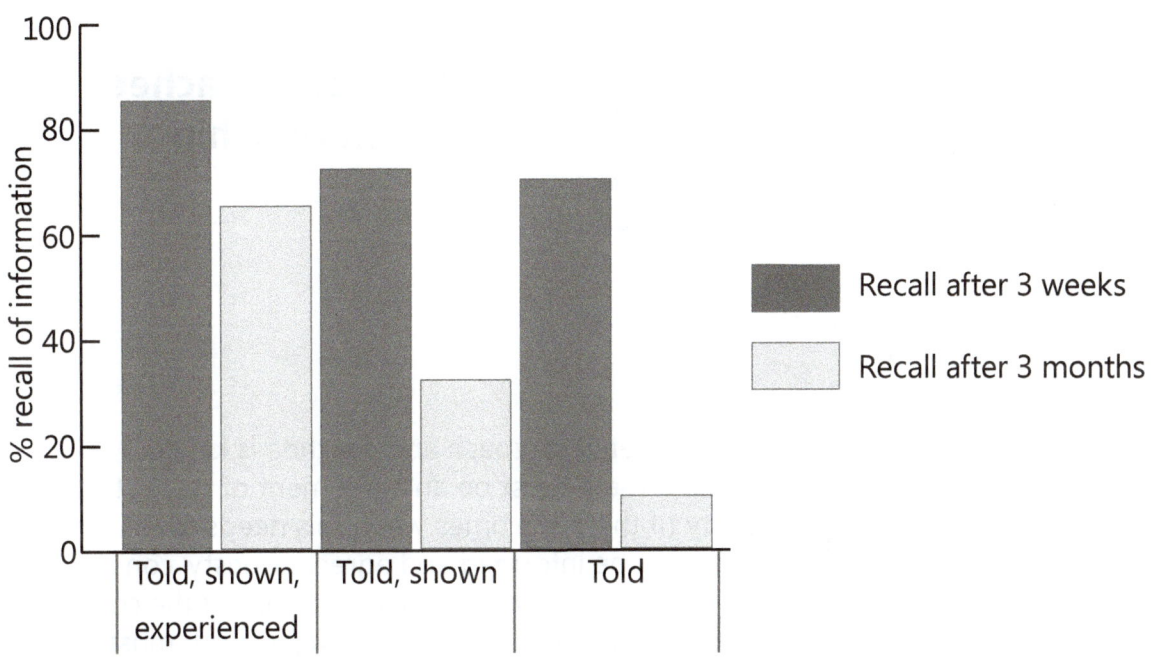

People are likely to be more motivated if they have the opportunity:

✓ To build their confidence, self-esteem and identity

✓ To have real responsibility and choice

✓ To experience a sense of making a real contribution and to be valued and appreciated.

questions create identity
choice create responsibility.

Asking, not telling raises awareness. Which is why an effective coach allows the coachee to identify their own areas for improvement and then develop their own strategy to achieve it.

!!!

The coach/coachee relationship

The relationship between coach and coachee is key to this process and there must be an agreement of respect, confidentiality (if there are times when this needs to be broken, the coachee must be informed and agree) honesty, congruence, genuineness and trust. If the coachee is unsure of the coach or vice-versa the process will not be effective, as both must feel free to be open, honest and be themselves.

The coach needs to follow a structured coaching plan. However, the coachee also needs to be open and willing to take part in the process, and want to learn and develop. If not, effective coaching will not be able to take place.

Sometimes a coachee may not show the desired requirements for coaching that we have described. For example someone may have been sent by their manager or someone else for coaching and do not personally wish to attend the session. They could show distrust, lack genuineness and congruence or even show disrespect. It must be made clear to them that in order for the coaching process to work and be effective they need to engage in the process and want to take part in the coaching sessions.

Any coachee who is not fully engaged is going to waste their time and yours so it is important to ascertain this at the beginning should you feel it may be an issue. It is perfectly ok to suggest to someone that they come back another time when they feel more ready as this may also be the gentle challenge they need to decide they are ready and show the required commitment to themselves and the process.

Coachees should be:

✓ Willing to take part in the process

✓ Understand the coaching process

✓ Have agreed to the basic principles of respect, confidentiality, honesty, trust, being non-judgmental, being genuine, having an open mind and integrity

✓ Self-motivated and willing to learn

✓ Committed to change and completing their goals

✓ Open to be challenged

✓ Open to look at things in a different way

✓ Able to accept responsibility for their own choice and actions, including how they have created their past and present

✓ Able to listen actively and consider appropriate feedback without being defensive or taking offence

✓ Able to consider others' views and beliefs without judgment

✓ Willing to try new things and take calculated risks

✓ Able to step out of their comfort zone

✓ Prepared to think outside the box and consider new concepts

✓ Accepting of their areas for development and able to praise themselves for their achievements

Ground rules

When a coach first meets a coachee, it's important to establish the ground rules for both parties. Some coaches draw up contracts or agreements documenting these ground rules and talk through them at the session with the coachee. Whether you wish to use a contract or just a discussion with the coachee, it's important that you discuss the following:

Confidentiality

You'll need to assure them that anything discussed in the session will remain confidential, and if you take notes how and where they're stored for security. Also, if you intend to discuss the notes or detail of the session with anyone else, e.g. a manager, a supervisor or group, or if the content will be used for appraisals and personal development plans, you must be sure that the coachee is aware of that before the session begins, and that you have their consent or permission to do so.

Timekeeping

Discuss whatever time frame you're working to, the consequences of a missed meeting or being late and also the time allocated to each session and its structure. You, as the coach, will be responsible for keeping to the allocated time.

Respect

Mutual respect is crucial, respect of timekeeping, beliefs, values, opinions, views and each others roles throughout the process.

Honesty

Being open and honest with each other will ensure the process works effectively. The coachee especially must be able to be honest with themselves and with you.

Being non-judgmental

The coachee must feel they are free to be and say what they wish without being judged. Equally, they need to be free from forming judgments about you as the coach and the coaching process.

Exercise: What extra ideas do you have for working with a coachee?

Structure of a coaching session

You can follow the following simple guide to the structure of a coaching session.

The three W's

Where are you now?

Establish a starting point – use the Life Areas Assessment or a version of it to help.

What are the issues/areas for development from where you are now?

Why are you where you are now – what have you done/not done?

Analyze the information without self judgment or blame – this is the starting point not an opportunity to beat yourself up!

What do you want?
Where do you want to be?

Identify the things you want and/or need.

Don't restrict yourself by getting caught up with the 'how' – just be free to explore all the things you would like if you could have anything you wished.

Start to form specific needs and wants from your ideas and prioritize the areas.

Consider whether what you want is positive and right for you and others around you – you can use the well formed outcome document discussed in sessions 4 and 5 for this.

What are you going to do about it?

Decide which goals you're going to work towards and complete sun diagrams (mini mindmaps which are featured in sessions 4 and 5) to establish the action points to achieve the goals.

Use the goal setting processes shown later in the program (sessions 4 and 5).

Commit to make the desired changes, and review and action the goals daily.

Remember:

✓ Coaching is enabling the coachee to do this for themselves, facilitating and supporting them through the process.

✗ Coaching is not doing this for the coachee, giving them the answers and instructing them.

Change and resistance

Coaching is all about change – as is, indeed, the whole of life. And yet change can be a huge stressor for most people – and any change, large or small, can create fear. That's because change is the unknown and can create fears of failure, of not being able to do something, or not being able to do it well or as well as others can.

illusion is good – learning process

This oh-so-human fear of failure comes from a desire to be accepted, liked and even loved, because when most people 'fail' they feel embarrassed, ashamed, silly or stupid.

don't feel that way IMPORTANT =>

Fear of change can send people spiraling into limiting belief patterns, worry and anxiousness. Actively resisting the change causes and spreads negative comments and attitudes.

Coaching point

Our belief systems often govern our reaction to change and how free we are to expand our comfort zone. When working as a coach, it's important to allow the coachee to look at all the options created by change and to encourage them to look at the positive outcomes possible to them. Looking at all the options often lets the coachee consider the worst possible outcome (which they will tend to do anyway) but also the best possible outcome and all areas in between.

Conversely, people who embrace change are generally very confident, free-feeling risk-takers who don't concern themselves with the concept of the possibility of failure.

Fearing and avoiding change will only serve to hold you back – and you could end up regretting the missed opportunities and experiences you might have enjoyed. So, whether you're self-coaching, working with a coaching partner or coaching your team at work, learning to embrace change is a fundamental goal.

"The quality of your life is directly related to the level of uncertainty you can comfortably tolerate", Anthony Robbins

The comfort zone

Understanding your comfort zone is the first step in understanding – and then dealing with – resistance to change.

Your comfort zone is the place where you're fully able, competent and comfortable. The job that you can do with your eyes shut or routines of life where you know exactly what you're doing. You may feel slightly challenged now and then, but nothing you can't easily handle.

It's when we're invited to step outside our comfort zone – or if we're pushed outside – that many of us react with resistance. After all, our beliefs tell us we might not be able to cope!

Everyday changes such as new computer or telephone systems, new staff, new jobs, new routines and procedures, new management, merging of departments, sections or whole companies or, on a personal level, exams, weddings, divorce, births, deaths, moving house and so on, are all high on the list of stressors due to change.

If you've got a rigid, limited comfort zone, you're going to be threatened by anything out of the ordinary. But we weren't born like that. Children don't have inhibitions and fears; it's only as we grow older that we learn to feel fear, that we learn what embarrassment is and how to feel silly or stupid – that is, we learn to have an ego.

This restricts our ability to have the freedom to learn, grow and be open to change, as we're nervous about asking questions for fear of looking silly, or trying new things for fear of failure, and we avoid doing anything that may cause us to feel embarrassed.

 Imagine what size a child's comfort zone must be, compared to an adult's!

And then think about this: if the limit of your comfort zone is something you've learnt, then you can learn to be more flexible and extend your boundaries. You're not constrained.

Get the most from anything in life:

- ✓ Open your mind
- ✓ Lose your inhibitions
- ✓ Be free of fear of failure
- ✓ Be who and what YOU want to be!

By being more fluid and open to change, accepting any fear and dealing with it effectively, you will not only grow your confidence and self-esteem, but you'll be free to develop your life with more happiness and less stress.

- ✓ Choose to flow with change rather than resist.
- ✓ Choose to challenge your comfort zone, pushing its limits further every day.
- ✓ Aim to have a comfort zone the size of a child's where nothing can faze or worry you, and you will notice a huge difference to the amount of things you are able to do and achieve in your life.

"The greatest discovery of my generation is that a human being can change their life by altering their attitude of mind."
William James

> **Remember** – the only failure is not trying again. If we fail at something at least we know what NOT to do next time!

Hidden issues

When coaching coachees won't always be free or feel free to give you all the information. For example, they may have something personal they don't want to discuss, or could even refuse to discuss, which is causing them issues or is a barrier to the goal they're trying to achieve.

Although performance coaching is based around the workplace, it's sometimes impossible to separate work from other areas of life, as they're all interlinked. For example, a person with issues in their home life may subconsciously bring them into work; or someone with health problems may experience difficulties in their relationships or finances, which could affect their work performance.

Workplace

Health   Family

Relationships   Finances

If you suspect there are hidden issues with your coachee, we recommend that you refer them to external help from an appropriate professional. This will clear the way for the coaching process to be effective.

It's very important that you remain within your boundaries. At the end of this program, you will have coaching skills but you will not be a qualified coach. So if you suspect your coachee needs specialized help they must be referred to a professional coach or therapist for help. Crossing such boundaries can actually cause more harm than good and create more pain or difficulty for the coachee. Never attempt to professionally coach or provide therapy for your team members or anyone else unless you are fully qualified to do so.

Understanding human behavior

When managing, teaching or coaching people, it's important to understand that we all have different learning and behavioral styles and different personality types. One style will not fit all, and to be successful in performance coaching you'll need to be flexible with your approach to suit each individual.

Exercise: Think of a skill you've learnt as an adult.

Spend a few minutes thinking about the stages you went through. Why did you decide to learn the skill?
How did you find out the information?
Who or what helped you to learn?
What didn't help?
How did you go from knowing nothing about the skill to being proficient at it?

Learning stages: ✓

1. Unconscious incompetence
   You don't know what you cannot do/do not know.

2. Conscious incompetence
   You know what you cannot do/know.

3. Conscious competence
   You know what you can do or think about it when doing it.

4. Unconscious competence
   You don't think about it, you just do it.

For example when you first start to learn to drive you start at level 1, you've seen other people do it and it looks easy enough, you are unconsciously incompetent. You don't even realize how hard the new skill will be to learn. As you have your first lesson where you kangaroo down the road, you become conscious of your incompetence (level 2). You learn over time and become competent but you are still thinking all the time about what you're doing (level 3). Finally after many hours of practise you reach the stage where you can drive the car without thinking of the mechanisms - you've now reached level 4 and become unconsciously competent.

As a coach you need to help people move through these levels. One of the difficulties can be identifying whether someone is at level 1 or 4, as in either case they will be confident of their ability to do the job. This is where your questioning skills really come into play (see later).

Sometimes you need, as a coach, to take someone from level 4 (unconscious competence) back down to the earlier levels in order for them to add extra dimensions to their skills.

Remember, if one human has done something then any human can do it if they want to, are committed enough to achieve it and are physically able to. This belief moves most people into the conscious competence phase; and even if they don't achieve the objective, they learn and continue to grow and develop.

The learning cycle: (David Kolb 1984)

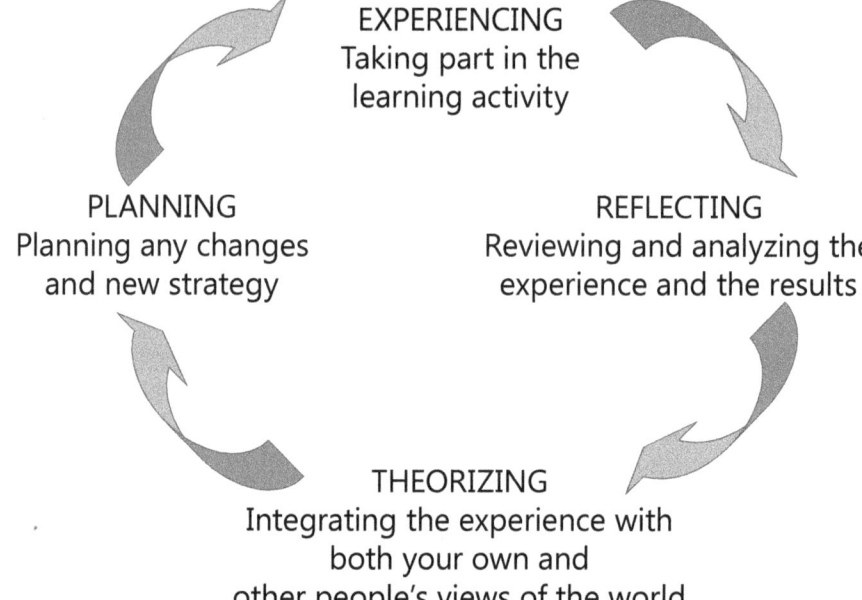

EXPERIENCING
Taking part in the
learning activity

REFLECTING
Reviewing and analyzing the
experience and the results

THEORIZING
Integrating the experience with
both your own and
other people's views of the world

PLANNING
Planning any changes
and new strategy

When working with coachees, you'll often find them in one or more phases of learning. The coaching process uses and encourages the flow of the experiencing–reflecting–theorizing–planning cycle as this is how we grow. From trying something, learning, making adjustments and applying that learning – life is about constant growth and change.

People have different strengths and weaknesses when it comes to the learning cycle and these can be identified using the four learning styles on the next few pages.

Learning styles – How do you learn best?

Peter Honey and Alan Mumford have identified four main learning style preferences, connected with the Kolb Cycle.

➢ Activist

➢ Reflector

➢ Theorist

➢ Pragmatist

Most of use a mixture of all four styles yet we'll lean towards a dominant style. We feel comfortable with one way of learning, our preferred learning style, and feel uncomfortable with others.

This can cause problems as styles can easily conflict, especially within the workplace. But learning to use all the styles gives you more choices, and access to more learning opportunities, and a good mix is healthy.

Activists:

Activists are generally seen as the go-getters and action orientated people. They tend to make quick decisions and don't like to be caught up in any form of detail. They are quick to delegate and don't have much patience with others who don't understand what they want quickly and efficiently. They often jump in at the deep end without thinking about the consequences.

Upside – they won't miss an opportunity; they're seen as confident and bold; they'll drive a project forward; and are often unafraid of change or taking risks.

Downside – they may make mistakes or poor decisions as they'll rush into things without considering all the options or issues; they can be impatient.

Reflectors:

Reflectors like to look at all the options and are the opposite of activists. They'll sit back and collect information and won't commit to making a decision until they've looked at all the information thoroughly. They tend to listen rather than speak.

Upside – they'll ensure they have the necessary information and make well-thought-out decisions so rarely make mistakes.

Downside – they take much longer to make decisions and won't make snap decisions, even under pressure. They can delay if they haven't got sufficient detail. They can be quiet, not the life and soul of the party. They don't tend to mix well with activists or vice versa as they're so different.

Theorists:

Theorists like to know the detail even more so than reflectors. They want to know the ins and outs of it all, how it works and what it's comprised of. They have a very rational outlook and love to debate theories and detail. If it's not rational it doesn't make sense and is therefore not to be considered. They are process-driven and very methodical in their approach.

Upside – they'll research projects and possibilities very thoroughly; they'll be intelligent and discuss issues in detail, with all the information to hand.

Downside – they'll take time to come to a decision and gather their conclusions without being rushed; they see no approach other than the rational approach and would find it difficult to work in an environment where fast talking and quick decision-making is required.

Pragmatists:

Pragmatists appear practical and rational and yet still like to get stuck in and do rather than reflect. They like things that they can see a benefit in and dislike too much detail or irrelevant information that takes up their time. Similar to activists, yet less hasty to jump in as they do need to see the reason and need some clarification that it's worth doing – they won't waste their time otherwise.

Upside – quicker in making decisions; will sift through for the facts; don't waste time; generally get on well with activists and add a bit more balance.

Downside – impatient if too much detail; will switch off in lengthy discussions as need to be kept occupied with variety; will rebel against anything they see as pointless or a waste of their time. Can appear to be dismissive and perhaps arrogant.

Source: Mumford, A. (1997) How to manage your learning environment. Peter Honey Publications.

To find out which style someone prefers you can complete an online learning styles questionnaire at www.peterhoney.com

Using the senses to learn

We also use our senses to learn and often we have preferences on which of our senses we tend to use as our primary style. In NLP they refer to the senses as VAK which covers three senses:

➢ Visual (to see)
➢ Auditory (to hear)
➢ Kinesthetic (to feel or sense)

There is also VAKOG and the OG are olfactory (to smell) and gustatory (to taste).

Some people learn more easily by being able to see things i.e. looking at pictures, diagrams or having handouts or presentations. Others may prefer to sit back and listen to information which means they are generally more auditory. Kinesthetic people will tend to learn more easily by experiencing something i.e. taking part, doing exercises and having a go at something they are learning.

Most people will use all of the styles and until you get to know them a little their dominant style may not be so obvious. So it is best to ensure you use all styles of sensory based learning to improve communication and learning. For example in presentations you can use visual aids, talk people through things and also get them to engage in exercises to try out their learning (VAK). You can also do this in a coaching session by using visual aids such as diagrams, draw pictures, use books or images and also ask the coachee to do the same or get them to listen to CDs or engage in trying things out and applying them. When you discover a coachee's preferred style you can engage with them more and set them relevant tasks which are also more suited to their preferences.

The following chart helps you to determine whether someone's primary learning style is visual, auditory or kinesthetic and tactile. The dominant system indicates your primary learning style. Most people rely on their primary learning style to communicate. Many people have a strong preference for two out of the three sensory styles.

Exercise: Which senses do you use?

For each row of the table allocate 5 marks between the 3 columns depending on how strongly the description matches yourself. E.g. If you feel the visual choice is most like you but the auditory a little bit then allocate 3 marks to the visual and 2 to the auditory. If on the next row only the visual was like you then give it all 5 marks.

When you	Visual	Auditory	Kinesthetic
Talk	Do you visualize and picture what you're discussing and say things like 'I see what you mean'?	Do you tend to listen more and be aware of the words? Do you say 'I hear what you're saying'?	Do you tend to say things like 'It feels right to me' and 'I have a handle on that now'?
Score			
Listen	Can you see and paint pictures of what people are saying when you listen? Do you add color and images to their words?	Do certain words stand out or you seem to hear them in different ways?	Are you moved to emotion easily when listening to music or when people talk about passionate subjects?
Score			
Make a decision	Do you have to have a specific vision and be able to see the outcome?	Do you speak to yourself (internally) considering all the options when decision-making as well as speaking openly with others?	Do you get a gut feeling when you're trying to make a decision when you know the right way to go?
Score			
Read	Can you visualize what you're reading, creating a story as you go along? Do you find it easy to read and see the words flow?	When you read, do you hear your voice or the character's voice in your head as you go along? Do you sometimes like to read out loud?	Do you find yourself experiencing the emotions of the characters and getting involved with the story as you go along?
Score			

When you	Visual	Auditory	Kinesthetic
Remember something	Can you see the event in your head like a movie?	Do you recall what was said as you hear it replayed?	Do you re-experience how you felt at the time?
Score			
Need help	Do you look for the solution or solutions with visual aids, lists or diagrams?	Do you ask for help and listen to others' suggestions? Do you repeat instructions back to yourself?	Do you ask for help and work with them or get them to show you as you go along? Do you feel you need to experience it to learn?
Score			
Do something new	Can you visualize and see in your mind how it will be? Do you read the instructions and look at pictures?	Do you talk yourself through how to do it? Do you ask someone to explain how to do it?	Do you prefer to work out how to do it rather than read instructions or be shown?
Score			
Teach someone	Do you show them, draw them a picture whilst you're explaining? Do you like to write it down for them?	Do you prefer to tell them how to do it, then let them do it?	Do you show them how to do it and ask them to join in with you at the same time?
Score			

	Visual	Auditory	Kinesthetic
Total score			
Preference			

Add up all the scores for each of the three senses. Then use the table below to assess your preference.

< 10	11-15	16-20	21-25	>25
least preferred	low preference	moderate preference.	high preference	dominant style

Individual and group dynamics – behavioral types

Transactional Analysis is a form of psychotherapy and is a useful tool for studying the behavior and personality of individuals and their affect on group dynamics.

You'll find being aware of group dynamics is essential for challenging any unwanted or negative patterns and positively changing attitudes, whether you're coaching individuals or whole teams.

I'm OK – You're OK

The 'I'm OK You're OK' principle (based on the original works of Eric Berne and discussed in the book 'I'm OK You're OK' by Thomas A Harris) describes a state of mind or judgment that someone makes, that could be conscious or subconscious. It's based on their belief of themselves and the world and can be very deep-rooted. Generally this behavior will be common in their whole life, not just their work.

People make sure that their 'map of the world' or perception is proved correct and will influence groups accordingly, either by being very positive and freely giving input to the group, striving to ensure its success; or by looking at things in a negative way, refusing to add value, instead behaving and commenting in negative destructive ways. They could be reluctant to bond with the team making it difficult for other team members or, worse still, influencing the attitude of the whole team.

warre

'I'm OK, You're OK':
This person is OK with themselves, their role and their situation and considers other people to be the same. Everything is great! The person is very positive, confident and open to new ideas and that's how they approach team work – positively influencing the team environment and adding value when and where they can.

'I'm Not OK, You're OK':
This person considers themselves to be less able, less competent and less skilled than others. They tend to be lacking in confidence and consider everyone else to be better than them so may have a fear of trying new things for fear that they fail or are measured against others. They don't really contribute much to a team as they prefer to sit quietly and observe, rather than make any voice their thoughts. These people need the maximum assurance through coaching to assist them to realize their true potential.

'I'm OK, You're Not OK':
This person considers themselves to be correct, effective in their role and happy with themselves, but makes judgments that others are perhaps not. They may be prone to gossiping and pointing the finger. When things go wrong, it's never their fault and they're likely to stand back rather than dig in to make things better. They're not a team player and don't really want to be. They'll be defensive if challenged, as they truly believe they are fine the way they are.

'I'm Not OK, You're Not OK':
This is a very negative person who doesn't think highly of themselves or others. Everything is always wrong and this person is inclined to moan and complain a lot, but won't have any solutions or be interested in trying anything. These people can often be wallowers and like to wallow in self-pity and negativity in every area of life. They are not team players and are not interested in others, as they reject them the same way as they reject and judge themselves.

	Feelings towards others	Communication	Accepting delegation
I'm OK You're OK	Always consider themselves to be equal to others and never look down on anyone..	They are able to communicate confidently and openly.	Delegate easily and accept delegation directed at them.
I'm Not OK You're OK	Always feel and see themselves as inferior.	They can be fearful of expressing their own opinion and prefer to ask others and let others make the decisions for them.	They will take instructions but may need reassurance that they can do it.
I'm OK You're Not OK	These people feel above everyone else and that they are superior.	They can be aggressive and arrogant and are often not interested in hearing others' views or opinions.	They avoid delegation and will question/ challenge whether someone else should do it instead if them.
I'm Not OK You're Not OK	These characters will appear withdrawn and disinterested in most things and can be seen as a loner.	They are often closed and defensive and generally feel they are being criticized.	They will reject instructions and delegation viewing it as they are being picked on or pushed around yet they tend not to challenge this.

Handling disagreement	Solving problems	Are moved to act
Consider the other person's opinion, see all sides and remain rational and calm.	Consider all the options and look for solutions believing there is always a solution.	Are able to motivate themselves and work alone or within a team.
Always keen to see something they have done wrong and will find evidence of this.	They will rely on others and need help as they feel they can't solve problems alone.	They tend to need lots of reassurance and hand holding.
They can create conflict and could bully.	Place blame on others, never themselves.	They are not self-motivated and often need to be forced or put under pressure to act.
They will tend to disagree with everything but offer no solutions.	They always seem to have problems they cannot solve and no-one else can help.	May need pushing, telling several times or even threatened at times, only acting when they really must.

Adapted from Thomas A Harris (1995)

Conscious perception

Conscious perception is about finding new ways of looking at an issue or goal to extend the coachee's choice and provide one or more motivating solutions.

Using the perceptual positions tool enables the coachee to see a wide variety of options, choices or differences by viewing the same problem, issue or situation from different angles.

1st position
is the position the coachee is as themselves, how they see, feel and experience things. Generally most people live their life in 1st position as their life is about them.

2nd position
is standing in someone else's shoes, trying to imagine how they feel about a situation or how it looks from their point of view.

This is effective when a coachee is struggling with something that involves someone else or when they're part of a team. It gently challenges them to see things from a different point of view, highlighting the positive or negative impact they can have without even knowing.

This position is often well practiced by 'people-pleasers' who always think of others and their impact on others before themselves.

3rd position
is like being a fly on the wall. The coachee is encouraged to look at the situation from a distance, as if they were looking in.

This is effective where emotions are running high, as it's a form of disassociation for the coachee. They're removed from their own thoughts and feelings and those of others, and asked to look in as an impartial observer. This is also a great tool to handle conflict and calm a situation.

Using the perceptual positions can be highly effective because when a coachee is encouraged to study a problem or issue from three different angles, it opens up their mind to many other possibilities. It allows them to consider other team members/ people without the need for direct challenge; i.e. they realize how they affect others without the coach or manager needing to point it out. This is a powerful tool to use when promoting change.

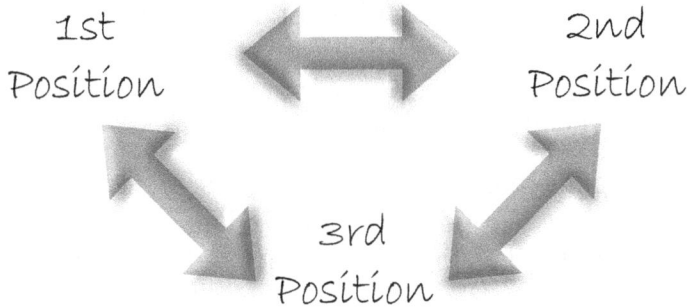

1st
Position

2nd
Position

3rd
Position

You can use this model for future or past situations. Encourage coachees to look back to identify how things could have been done differently and what solutions they would now apply; or to look forward and consider how best to approach a future challenge or situation.

When using perceptual positions to help with conflict, you can consider the concept of positive intent and ask the coachee to look for the positive intent from others' comments or actions in the 2nd and 3rd position.

If they look hard enough, they can see a good intention in anything, which will dissipate their negative emotions, allowing them to seek rational solutions more easily.

> The 51% rule is useful with conflict resolution. If a coachee is in conflict with a co-worker or anyone else, ask them to consider that they are 51% responsible for a situation. If they can accept that they're 51% responsible for a situation, they'll be more open to taking action to resolve it rather than hitting stalemate, which is counter-productive to all.

Behaviors and beliefs –
assertive, aggressive and submissive

Assertive

Assertion is a behavior and way of being that is well balanced and rational. It is standing up for your own rights without the need to violate the rights of others. It is being respectful of others but also expressing openly your thoughts and opinions confidently and without concern or judgments.

Assertive people express their needs, wants, feelings, opinions and beliefs in direct, honest and appropriate ways. For some, assertion has to be developed and practiced and is a skill that can be developed.

Aggressive

Aggression is generally an inappropriate behavior especially within the workplace. There are rare times where it is called for but it is often deemed to be an inappropriate behavior. Aggression can violate the rights of others especially if it creates fear and can be seen as bullying.

Aggressive people are likely to ignore or dismiss others' needs, opinions, and feelings.

This type of behavior needs to be controlled and challenged and changed quickly.

Submissive

Submissive people are often seen as shy and generally find themselves being overlooked, not considered or not included in decision making or general company development issues.

Submissive managers are often ineffective and don't command respect. These characters tend not to stand up for themselves, their rights and even others. When they do say something it is often ignored or disregarded quickly and they will not challenge this, rather tend to agree.

They tend not to express their needs, opinions and feelings or do so in an apologetic manner.

The following table provides information on how each of these styles tend to be displayed either via body language, facial expressions, the pace and tone of voice and eye contact. This will help you have awareness of how you may be perceived by others and also gauge what style your coachee tends to behave like generally or in certain situations.

	Assertive People
Body	Stand and speak in a confident and relaxed fashion. Give good eye contact and smile a lot. Generally speak at a good pace and reasonable volume without needing to shout. Have a rational, balanced and easy feel about them. Use open gestures with hands and arms. Firm but not crushing handshake.
Facial	Genuine smiles and smile a lot. Use open and friendly expressions in a confident and at ease manner.
Voice	Rational and controlled, confident and self-assured with a good pitch and volume, even-paced, firm, warm, sincere, encouraging and clear. Happy to speak to listen.
Pace	Good and moderate pace which is easy to understand. Relevant humor and content for the situation. Steady and confident open communication for all.
Eye contact	Natural and relaxed showing a friendly nature and putting others at ease. Enough but not too much eye contact.

Aggressive People	Submissive People
Can often invade other peoples' space without showing any respect. Like to be in the center of everything. Do a lot of finger pointing and can have a strong if not crushing handshake trying to assert their dominance. Ensure their presence is known and act over-confident. Lots of body movement and gestures to attract attention to show themselves as powerful.	Tend to look down and avoid eye contact with others. Demonstrate a shy and lacking in confidence body posture with hunched shoulders and back, they don't stand tall with their head held high. Speak with their hand over their mouth feeling uncertain they are saying the right thing and may stutter or speak quietly. Generally have a weak or overly gentle handshake.
When they smile which will not be too much, they often don't appear genuine or can seem patronizing. Scowl or frown with lips and jaw appearing tight.	Generally smile to please and check that others are OK with them. Can have nervous twitches, look down, blush easily, chew their lip or hide their mouth with their hand.
Can be loud, tendency to be sarcastic and interrupt a lot. Will shout to be the center of attention and can easily switch to being defensive and angry if ignored or challenged.	Gentle and quiet non assuming voice. If challenged or put on the spot can be shaky and hesitant, unsure or may even say nothing.
Loud and fast, abrupt and erratic. Loud laugh to attract attention and if not at the center will interrupt or speak louder and faster to regain control.	Slow pace with lots of hesitation and 'ers'. Avoid talking at all if can. Nervous laughter, if feeling under pressure. Possible stuttering, throat clearing, disjointed sentences.
Can glare and give intimidating stares to try to control and dominate. Can appear threatening.	Generally avoid all eye contact if they can. Look down and occasionally look up very briefly. Will talk, but look in other direction.

Coaching dos and don'ts

Do:

- ✓ Abide by the coaching ground rules (see earlier).

- ✓ Maintain confidentiality and inform the coachee of times when this may be broken.

- ✓ Be honest, genuine, congruent, show empathy to coachee's feelings, be non-judgmental and respectful at all times.

- ✓ Demonstrate active listening by truly listening to all the details (don't let your mind wander) and show the coachee you are listening via body language and facial expressions to create and maintain rapport.

- ✓ Give constructive feedback.

- ✓ Challenge when appropriate.

- ✓ Be honest and open and encourage the coachee to challenge themselves, too.

- ✓ Summarize frequently to make sure you've got the correct information and to maintain control of the session.

Don't:

✗ Judge in any way. Ensure you put your own beliefs and values to one side and maintain an open mind to suggestions without immediately dismissing them as impractical or worthless. Stay objective.

✗ Discuss yourself. Self-disclosure can sometimes help a coachee but generally is not a good thing. Ensure the session remains about the coachee, as it's their time.

✗ Lose track of time. You are in control of the session and keeping track of time.

✗ End the session abruptly. If the coachee is likely to be or becomes upset towards the end of the session, you need to leave time to show empathy and ensure they are okay. It is not appropriate to rush them off as soon as the session has finished. You must ensure they're okay before they leave.

✗ Take phone calls or allow the session to be interrupted. Clearly, the coachee will be talking about personal issues as well as business, and the session needs to be private, without interruptions or distractions. Your phones should be diverted, and all mobiles should be turned off – including the coachee's.

Will you be a good coach?

Exercise: See how many of the following you can agree with. Any you don't currently do, or would disagree with, may need some development.

- ❑ I offer help without taking over, I do not advise or tell people what to do as they can find the solution for themselves.
- ❑ I involve others in decision making and encourage people to contribute and keep open-minded about their contributions.
- ❑ I express my opinion but also listen to others.
- ❑ I help people to get clarity and set achievable goals for them.
- ❑ I encourage people to ask questions of themselves and others.
- ❑ I ensure people are valued for themselves and their skills, and encourage them to equally value themselves.
- ❑ I give frequent and honest feedback on performance.
- ❑ I reward, praise and give recognition focusing on what is done well rather than not so well.
- ❑ I encourage people to try new things and new ways of doing things. I believe there is always a solution.
- ❑ I see mistakes and failure as learning what not to do next time and how to improve and develop.
- ❑ I cultivate an environment of trust, support and understanding.
- ❑ I believe people have more skills than they use at work.
- ❑ I am non-judgmental with people, regardless of their beliefs religion and background.

Coaching corner

Using and identifying sensory learning during a coaching session

One of the great skills required by a coach is to identify the coachee's preferences which I like to call to be able to speak their 'psychological language'. Understanding the different styles such as Sensory Learning (which is also referred to as VAK or VAKOG in NLP) is a way of adapting to the coachee to use similar language to them or ways of presenting information or examples to them which they can understand easily and quickly. Adapting the session around their sensory style allows the session to be more effective whilst building upon the coachee coach relationship.

Coachees will use many references to their preferred senses using specific language and also physical movements with their body and hands during the session which allow the coach to identify their style. Examples of this could be the coachee saying things like, 'I see what you mean', 'let me paint you a picture of what I'm saying', 'It looks right', or they may use their fingers and hands to create pictures or visual signs as they speak. All of these would be the traits of visual people. For a coach to adapt they would need to use visual words back and also describe things in a visual way using their body language and hands or even using paper to write and draw information and next steps etc. using every visual aid possible. They may even ask the coachee to create visual tools to assist them or ask them to create homework using visual aids rather than just discussion. All of this will be very comfortable for the coachee as it is their 'style' and a more effective way for coaching, development and learning for them.

If a coachee was more auditory they may use language like, 'I hear what you are saying', 'It sounds good to me', 'It's like a buzzing in my head'. These coachees will like to listen a lot more and find it easier to concentrate by just listening as visual aids can tend to distract them. The coach needs to adapt by using extra material that they could listen to such as CDs or DVDs if appropriate and allow the coachee to talk and listen, keeping it simple and keeping other aids to a minimum. The coach would also ensure they use similar auditory language by using similar words to the coachee such as 'how does that sound?'

Kinesthetic coachees are all about feelings, whether they be internal i.e. they feel happy/sad/hot/cold or external i.e. the chair is heavy, the table feels smooth etc. These coachees will talk more about how things make them feel and use language such as, 'It just doesn't feel right', 'I can't get a handle on it', 'I don't get it', 'The penny has dropped'. These coachees will tend to look downwards more when talking and the coach will need to get them to look up more to break any patterns if they are talking about negative emotions a lot, looking up at the coach rather than downwards can help them to break the pattern of negative feeling and open them to being more resourceful (this is discussed more in session 3).

We all use all of our senses and coachees can mix them in conversation such as, 'I can't see the way forward, it feels too hard right now'. This coachee would be using visual and kinesthetic sensory language which is common yet they will have a preference of a style they use more often, especially when under pressure and if the coach listens and looks out for the signs they will easily be able to identify this and adapt to use that style more with the coachee, ensuring they talk their coachees 'psychological language' and learning style to create a more effective coaching session.

If in doubt and you really don't think you have identified a specific style then it is also easy to integrate all 3 styles in any session and therefore ensure that you are able to match them in different ways.

Notes page

Personal reflection –
How to use the perceptual positions

Perceptual positions may be a useful tool to use if you ever find yourself at a stalemate with someone, each believing yourselves to be correct or perhaps you need to consider how your behavior may impact upon others.

When using this tool for yourself it is useful to sit down and relax first. Find a quiet space where you will not be interrupted by people or telephones and consider the points below. It is also useful to get someone to work with you, asking you the questions one by one with pauses so you can think about them. You do not need to answer with this exercise as all of the work is done privately in your own head and you will be surprised how you may see things differently and have strong emotions or feelings that perhaps you were not aware of previously. Make sure that you take your time and really see and consider the answers to each of the questions before moving on. This is a very powerful exercise and you may be not like some of the feelings and emotions that are raised for you so make sure you do this exercise in a safe environment for you.

Imagine that you are there now, the situation or event you wish to work on.

What do you see? Feel? Hear? What impact is it having on you? What would you change or do differently?

Now imagine you are the other person/people as if you were standing in their shoes.

How do you now see the situation or event? Does it look different? Feel different? Do you hear anything different?

What are the changes/differences you are observing and what impact do they have upon you as them in their shoes i.e. how does it feel to be them having to deal with you or react to you? What would you like to do differently as them and what would you now like to do?

Finally imagine someone is observing both of you but from a distance like a fly on the wall or a stranger walking by and watching and hearing the situation or event.

What do they see? What do they hear? How do they feel about it? What impact does it have on them? What do they think should be done differently and what would they like to do?

Now go back to position 1 and consider if you would make any changes after experiencing all 3 positions and gaining new insight from using this powerful tool.

Another way to do this exercise is to physically move from chair to chair or move into different places to stand, with your eyes open but still imagining the different positions and perspectives.

Session 3

Coaching Skills Toolbox

"Nobody can do everything,
but everyone can do something."

Session 3

Coaching skills toolbox

Objectives for session 3:

**When you've worked through this session,
you should be able to:**

- ✓ Explain why establishing rapport is so important in coaching

- ✓ Match and mirror people's body language

- ✓ Recognize different eye accessing cues when you speak to people

- ✓ Describe the difference between open and closed questions and say when and why you'd use them

- ✓ Summarize a conversation clearly, accurately and succinctly

- ✓ Give positive feedback effectively

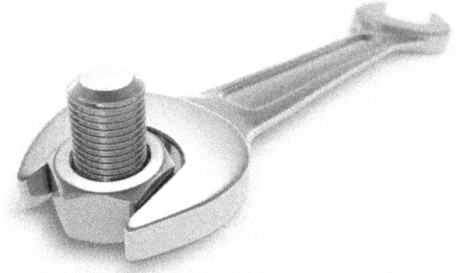

Tools in session 3:

- ✓ Matching and mirroring – used to build rapport with your coachee.

- ✓ Eye accessing and VAK – used to be able to assess what information coachees are accessing and which sensory styles or emotions they are using.

- ✓ Questioning – the best ways to ask questions to gain information or a commitment.

- ✓ Summarizing – to maintain rapport, showing you are listening and understanding, keep control of the session and also ensure you understand the situation.

- ✓ Feedback – how to give positive feedback to motivate action for positive change.

Building and establishing rapport

Rapport is something many people already have without even knowing it. It's a way of connecting with someone and feeling a bond, or liking them and feeling at ease with them but perhaps not knowing why.

Have you ever met someone and taken an instant dislike to them – even before you've spoken to them?
You don't know why, but you just don't like the look of them?
And you don't like how you feel around them?
This is because you both haven't connected and established rapport (consciously and unconsciously).

Have you ever met someone and immediately felt like you've known them forever and you really like them?
You have rapport with this person.

Sales people are aware of this and learn the skill of building rapport quickly and making sure they maintain it as, after all, we often buy because we like the person as well as the product. We rarely buy from someone if we don't like them.

Theory:

✓ People like people who are like themselves.

✓ We like people who are like us.

✓ I like people who are like me.

Rapport can be built unconsciously – as many sales people will do – and doesn't need to be focused on words. It's often a similarity or something 'like us' or 'a match' that makes the connection. Body language plays a huge part, as do the words you use, even down to how you say them.

When communicating, especially when presenting to a group or teaching, the actual words used are only part of your message. When miscommunication occurs, research has shown that only 7% of the listener's attention is on what the person is saying, 38% is focused on how they are saying it and a massive 55% of the listener's attention is on the speaker's body language.

Physiology

➢ Posture

➢ Movements – head, body, hands

➢ Gestures

➢ Facial expression

➢ Breathing

➢ Shoulders – position, tension

Voice

➢ Tone – pitch

➢ Tempo – speed

➢ Timbre – quality

➢ Rhythm – cadence

➢ Volume – loudness

Language

➢ Content and form

➢ Organizational words

➢ Professional words

➢ Sensory language

Establishing rapport is vital to the success of any coaching session. Without it, the coachee is unlikely to make the progress they want. Some people are naturally able to build rapport and others struggle, but the good news is that you can build rapport with someone even if you're not a natural.

Here are some sample rapport-builders and indicators that rapport has been established.

Matching & Mirroring

Match: Do the same – if they have their leg crossed to the right, you cross your leg to the right

Mirror: Do the opposite, as in a mirror – if they have their leg crossed to the right, you cross yours to the left. This style is less obvious

Micro-match: If they cross their leg at the knee to the right, you cross your leg at the ankle to the right, or cross your hands if they fold their arms – anything similar, but a lesser movement.

Micro-mirror: If they cross their leg at the knee to the right, you cross your leg at the ankle to the left or cross your hands if they fold their arms – anything similar but a lesser movement and the opposite direction.

Macro-match: If they cross their leg at the ankle to the right, you cross your leg at the knee to the right – anything similar but a greater movement.

Macro-mirror: If they cross their leg at the ankle to the right, you cross your leg at the knee to the left – anything similar but a greater movement and the opposite direction.

People in rapport tend to match or mirror each other unconsciously.

People not in rapport mismatch each other.

Here are some of the ways to build rapport:

Physiology

Standing, leaning or sitting in a similar way to the person, crossing your legs, folding arms, holding pen in same hand, using and respecting the same spatial distances, using the same body language as they naturally move and change their posture.

Following their facial expressions by smiling at the same time as them or looking concerned if that is how they look.

Being aware of their breathing. You can help someone calm down by matching and pacing their breath – matching their breathing (the speed) and then slowing your breath down to help them naturally (and unconsciously) follow you, having a calming effect. This needs practise to be natural and not obvious, but is a great skill to have.

Eye accessing – following and matching their eye cues and patterns. People tend to look up to the right or left or down or to the side when accessing different parts of their brain and memory. If you can match or mirror this, it's one of the less obvious styles of rapport building – we cover this in more detail later in the program.

Voice

Being aware of and matching their voice tone, volume, pitch and speed is a skill that sales people often use, especially when trying to sell to people over the telephone. If someone speaks slowly it's a good style to slow your speech down slightly to try to match them (but not obviously) especially if you're generally a fast speaker, and vice-versa if speaking to a fast talker. Remember, we like people who are like ourselves, and voice tone gives rich communication. We've all experienced someone whose voice we don't like and we just switch off and stop listening. Equally we've all experienced listening to someone who keeps us held like a magnet, hanging on their every word. Do you think this is just lucky for them or do you think they've worked on this as a skill?

Words

Words are still important and using similar words will build rapport. Try having a conversation with a trendy teenager who uses lots of 'street jargon' just to see what a mismatch words can be! Or consider using very positive language with a person who is often very negative. They'll find your words irritating as they don't match their language.

Once you have an idea of the type of language and words a person uses, you can adapt to match them a little more. Most people tend to do this, anyway.

Listen to the words people use and assess whether they tend to be more positive or negative. Be aware of the words you choose to use too, as your words will influence you and others.

Examples of negative words:

Abnormal, argue, can't, difficult, disaster, doubt, error, failure, hopeless, lazy, lose, ought, problem, should, useless, but, mistake.

Examples of positive words:

Achievement, build, congratulate, consider, create, encourage, grow, help, improve, new, plan, promote, sincere, solve, strong, succeed, support, thank you, thoughtful, valuable, learning, please, opportunity.

How do you communicate?

Look at the following letters. How would you split them? Which is it for you?

OPPORTUNITYISNOWHERE

OPPORTUNITY IS NOWHERE

OPPORTUNITY IS NOW HERE

If you're working through this program alone, take every opportunity to practice building and improving your rapport-building skills. You can use these in every area of your life and you can also now coach others on how to improve their skills, too. Often, if there's conflict or problems with teams bonding, these skills can help and you can now observe where the mismatches lie.

If you're working through this program with a colleague, you can use the following exercises to improve your rapport-building skills. You can also use these exercises to coach and teach others about rapport.

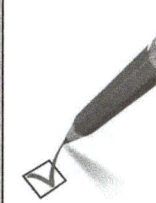

Exercise: Rapport building

Find a partner and practice building rapport.

Person A: Talk about what you did last weekend for two minutes whilst changing your body posture, facial expressions, tone and pace of voice as described in the micro/macro matching and mirroring section. (Exaggerate this and change posture every few seconds).

Person B: Build and maintain rapport by matching (micro/macro) and mirroring (micro/macro) within a few seconds of your partner moving.

This will be obvious and unnatural, but it's a good way to gain the skills and practise. You can then refine it for the real thing.

Then swap and repeat with Person A attempting to build and maintain rapport, and Person B talking for two minutes.

See how it feels to build and maintain rapport.

Exercise: Mismatch

Repeat the exercise, with A and B taking turns to talk about what they're going to do next weekend for two minutes but this time deliberately mismatching i.e. breaking rapport with the speaker.

Mismatch all the postures your partner adopts – i.e. do the opposite to what you did in the first exercise. You are deliberately getting the skills wrong to break rapport.

See how it feels to break or not establish rapport.

Body language, psychogeography, eye cues

Body language

A coachee's body language tells its own story in a coaching session and you can observe changes in their language to indicate how they're feeling.

A coachee will sit differently when they're relaxed from when they're anxious. Think about yourself and how you hold your body when you're tense. How do you sit, stand and walk? When you're relaxed, how do you sit, stand and walk? When you're angry, how does your body language change? What do you do with your arms or legs, and what is your facial expression like?

Body language is hugely important – but don't fall into the trap of making assumptions about how a person is feeling or what they're thinking just from looking at their body language. Everyone is not the same.

You may think someone looks cross – but they might be concerned. You may think someone looks bored – but they might be thinking about what you just said. You may think someone looks confused – but they might be processing information and be deeply interested in the subject.

Guessing what a person is thinking or feeling is called 'mind reading' and is to be avoided in a coaching session. If you want to know what a coachee is thinking or feeling it's best to ask.

Psychogeography and its boundaries

Where you sit or stand in relation to anyone makes a statement and sends them different signals. These signals can be unconscious so we might not consciously recognize them.

With some people, we may feel safe or happy to be around them so we consciously and unconsciously include them within our boundaries; but other people feel strange or different to us so we exclude them from our boundaries.

This is a useful concept to be aware of because we can learn and choose to include or exclude people from our boundaries, to build or break rapport at will to allow us to feel a sense of belonging and safety.

With psychogeography (personal space or spatial awareness) you need to be aware of and consider:

➢ The spatial distance between you and your coachee or the person you're talking to

➢ The angle of your face to theirs

➢ The angle of your body to theirs

➢ The other person's space (personal boundaries)

➢ Your own personal space (your boundaries)

Eye accessing cues

Eye accessing cues are another form of body language used to help the coaching process.

They are the movements people make with their eyes when they're processing information, thinking or remembering. They can be used to assess what part of their mind and senses the coachee is accessing to answer your question or to consider a statement. They can help you be sure that your coachee is being congruent with their feelings and genuine with their answers. You can also use them to allow the coachee more time when they're accessing, constructing or remembering information.

A high percentage of the population uses the same eye accessing pattern when remembering or constructing information. Police also use some of these skills (plus others) to determine whether a person is lying.

It's important to remember that we don't all follow the same pattern and for some people, the pattern is completely reversed (approximately 80% of people follow this pattern, left handed people are often reversed and some people have a very different pattern altogether), so a certain amount of calibration is required (checking whether the pattern is standard or reversed) before it can be used effectively to judge if people are telling the truth or not! We don't advise you to use it for this purpose. These skills are used to help maintain rapport and gain a better understanding of your coachee, not to analyze whether they're telling the truth.

For around 80 per cent of the population, the following may apply:

If a person looks to the left when answering a question (your left as you're looking at them) they might be constructing information. For example, they could be thinking how it might sound, feel, hear or taste. This is also where people could look if they were lying, as they'd be constructing information, i.e. making it up.

When someone looks to the right they are generally remembering information they have experienced or know.

Visual is what we see or remember seeing.

Auditory is what we hear or remember hearing or talk to ourselves in our mind, our inner dialog.

Kinesthetic is what we feel in terms of emotions or also physical touch and pleasure or pain.

Internal dialog is what we say to ourselves.

To help use this tool - if a person follows the most likely pattern then as you look at them imagine a giant C curving round their head. This side will be the constructed thoughts (your left).

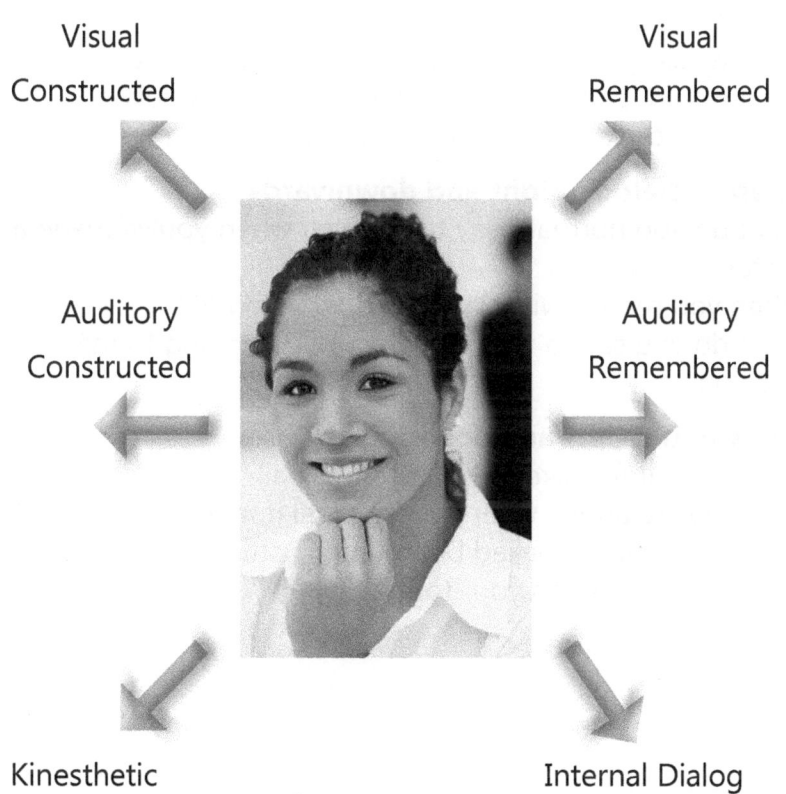

Visual	Visual
Constructed	Remembered
Auditory	Auditory
Constructed	Remembered
Kinesthetic	Internal Dialog

Here are some examples of where people will generally look when asked different questions:

Visual remembered – right and upwards
What color is your favorite jumper?
What did your first pair of shoes look like?
What's the most beautiful city you've ever visited?

Visual constructed – left and upwards
What do you get if you spell the word 'stop' backwards?
Imagine the sky turning bright purple with green clouds.
How would your mother look with a Mohican hairstyle?

Auditory remembered – right and to the side
Who shouts the loudest in your family?
What does your favorite childhood song sound like?
What's the funniest ring tone you've ever had on your mobile?

Auditory constructed – left and to the side
What would your friend sound like reciting poetry?
What would it sound like if a dog could do karaoke?
What would an elephant sound like if it snored?

Internal dialog – right and downwards
What do you normally say to yourself when you've made a mistake?
When you reason with yourself, do you say 'I'?
What do you say to yourself when you're trying to make a decision?

Kinesthetic – left and downwards
What does it feel like to hold a snow ball?
When you're angry, where do you feel it in your body?
If you were eating baked beans and custard at the same time, how would it feel on your tongue?

Listening and questioning

Good listening and questioning skills are essential to being a good coach.

Open questions are used when you want to get information from the coachee.

These types of questions start with words such as:

✓ WHAT?

✓ WHERE?

✓ WHEN?

✓ HOW?

✓ WHO?

WHY is not commonly used when coaching, as 'why' often encourages the coachee to tell a story or go into past detail that isn't relevant to the coaching process.

'Why' questions are used a lot in therapy and tend to be avoided in a coaching situation.

Closed questions are effective when you want to gain commitment from a coachee. These types of questions get a 'yes' or 'no' answer and can be used for clarification.

Such questions would start with words like:

✓ DO

✓ IS

✓ HAVE

✓ CAN

✓ IF

The following is a good exercise to use with a group when explaining about the use of questioning skills. The exercise demonstrates how using closed questions takes a long time to gain accurate information and open questions can be far more effective.

If you use this exercise for a group or even an individual, mark down how many closed questions it takes them to guess what you have drawn. They only need one question when asking open questions – 'what have you drawn?'

Exercise: Questioning
Draw a picture, making sure that the other person can't see it.
The other person is allowed to use only closed questions to guess what you've drawn on your piece of paper.
Note how many questions were asked to get the answer.
Draw a second picture.
Now let the other person use open questions to guess what else you've have drawn on your piece of paper.
Note how many questions were needed this time.

Sample questions for coaching

To start the session:
➢ What do you feel we need to focus on?
➢ What is it you want to achieve?
➢ Where shall we start?
➢ So, how can I help?
➢ What are the key issues you wish to address?

To challenge:
➢ How else could you achieve it?
➢ How else could you view the situation?
➢ What makes you think that?
➢ What are your thoughts about?
➢ What do you mean by...?
➢ What are you going to do?
➢ How else could it work out?

To gain more information and clarity:
➢ What are more examples of this?
➢ What specifically do you mean by...?
➢ For what purpose?
➢ You may not know right now but, if you did know ...,
  what would it be?
➢ How might someone else solve this?
➢ What else do you need to consider?

To get commitment to achieve/change:

➢ So what are you going to do?

➢ How will you know when you have it?

➢ When you get it, what will you see, hear and feel?

➢ What will happen if you do...?

➢ If you don't..., what will that do for you?

➢ What effect will this change have on others?

➢ How willing are you to...?

➢ How will you make time to...?

➢ By when will this happen?

Listening

When listening to a coachee, it's important to listen attentively and not to be concerned about thinking of your next question or, even worse, letting your mind wander.

Coachees can allude to issues or give hints of trouble they have without actually saying it, and by actively listening the coach can pick up on things that even the coachee wasn't aware they were saying or meaning.

The old saying that we have one mouth and two ears and we should use them in that same ratio is a very good lesson when coaching, as listening to the answer to the questions is far more important and revealing than speaking yourself.

Silences can be very effective too and it's important that the coach doesn't feel the need to fill a silence. Often if the coachee isn't speaking, they're thinking, and interrupting that thought pattern could prevent some important learning taking place.

Angus McLeod's Three Principle Instruments of Coaching teaches how to ask questions, challenge the answers and then use silence to allow the coachee to increase their conscious perception of the issue.

For example, if the coach asks the coachee 'What stopped you from applying for the job?', the coachee could say, 'Because I always fail to get every job I apply for'. The coach challenges this statement by saying, 'Every job?' and is then silent.

The coachee automatically backtracks to consider if they had actually failed at every job they'd had ever applied for – which of course wouldn't be true as they're in a job now, so must have passed at least one job interview.

They'd be forced to 'reframe' that belief in their head as they'd just proved to themselves it was untrue. They could then consider the possibility that, actually, they could pass a job interview, having done it once already!

Summarizing and reframing

Summarizing is an important part of coaching and is used for many reasons. It is another good rapport-builder, as it demonstrates that the coach is listening and understanding and offers a way to gain a better understanding of the situation or issue.

A summary is usually a shortened, concise version of an original conversation and does not usually repeat all the detail. The coach reviews the conversation, recalling the key issues discussed.

Summaries contain key words used by the coachee, and might also rephrase or reorder information.

Why summarize?

✓ To clarify and to make sure you have the correct understanding of the situation

✓ To demonstrate you're listening and want to check you have all the information you require

✓ To build and maintain rapport

✓ To give the coachee the chance to correct or add to the key issues

✓ To redirect the conversation back to the key issue

✓ To look at the situation differently

✓ To break a pattern of behavior or emotion

✓ To take control of the conversation and conclude

✓ To help the coachee to get back on track if they lose their train of thought

✓ To challenge the coachee

Examples of how to summarize

- ➢ Can I just take a moment to run through the details to ensure I fully understand them?

- ➢ Just let me summarize this for a moment. You've been talking about...

- ➢ Let me check I've got all the details...

- ➢ So what I think you're saying is...

- ➢ So I'm hearing that you...

- ➢ We've been discussing how you ...

- ➢ So, you think that...?

- ➢ So the main points we need to consider are... is that right or have I missed anything?

- ➢ I'm not sure I understand the issue fully, can we just quickly run through the main points again?

- ➢ Just take a moment whilst I check I understand all that we've discussed: you said that...

- ➢ Okay, so from today's session we have decided that...

- ➢ You have covered a lot of information, can I just double check I fully understood it all?

- ➢ So the next steps for you will be... is that correct?

Positive feedback

> Effective coaching requires positive feedback –
> not negative criticism.
>
> Feedback should be positive, constructive and motivational

Whether you're a coach, a manager, a leader or a friend, learning to give appropriate feedback is a skill that will benefit you in any area of life.

Giving effective feedback is about providing useful information in a positive and constructive way so that the person can use that information to improve their behavior or skills and still feel good about what they've heard, i.e. they don't feel upset, defensive or ignore what has been offered to them.

A good way to offer feedback is to ask for the individual's personal reflection first before providing your opinion/feedback.

This is far more empowering for the individual as they then take ownership of their comments rather than just being given information from you. If we have an idea or belief about something we tend to take it far more seriously than being given the idea by someone else, especially if that person is your manager.

Roger Leadbeater kindly offered his tool for giving effective feedback which he has called 'The 2 C's'. He believes in allowing for personal reflection first, followed by feedback coaching. He states that managers' feedback gives you 'Compliance' whereas self-feedback gives us 'Commitment', i.e. the person is committed to positive change rather than feeling they need to comply with it. I find that this technique works well and is highly effective as it also encourages ideas and empowers the individual to take charge of their own growth and development.

Effective feedback

When giving feedback, give it in a positive sandwich;

- ✓ Say something positive about the situation
- ✓ Followed by the area which could be improved
- ✓ End with another positive comment

When giving feedback

- ✓ Prepare what you're going to say before you say it
- ✓ Be specific, not vague. Say exactly what happened – 'it didn't seem to work when you said xyz' rather than 'it didn't work'
- ✓ Own your statements using 'I' – 'I think...' or 'In my opinion...'
- ✓ Focus on observed behavior – not on personality
- ✓ Describe events factually and not from feelings
- ✓ Refer to behaviors that can be changed
- ✓ Offer positive alternatives – not just criticism
- ✓ Leave the coachee knowing what's been achieved and what they want to achieve
- ✓ Leave the coachee agreeing what is to be done differently
- ✓ Most of all, leave the coachee motivated

Make certain the coachee understands that they have a role too, and they need to:

✓ Listen

✓ Avoid being defensive or aggressive

✓ Ask for examples and seek clarification

✓ Look for mutual ways forward

✓ Be prepared to accept changes where possible

Remember this ...

Feedback:

✓ Focuses on the behavior, skill or the situation – not the person

✓ Is specific

✓ Is timely

✓ Is always positive

✓ Seeks a solution or options

✓ Results in the person feeling motivated to change/grow/ feel good

✓ Focuses on positive issues (for things done well) as well as the negative (things to improve upon)

✓ Should always be a positive sandwich!

Examples of how to and how not to give feedback:

Feedback focuses on the behavior, skill or the situation – not the person

I found how you said it sounded a little critical.

NOT You sounded critical.

Feedback is specific

I think the last 5 slides of the presentation need more detail.

NOT I want you to change the presentation.

Feedback is timely

When you went through the report in the meeting this morning I felt you seemed a little negative.

NOT When you went through the report last week I felt you seemed a little negative.

Feedback is always positive

I loved the article. You're getting really good at writing them.

NOT You're making fewer mistakes these days.

Feedback seeks a solution/options

I really like your ideas, very inspirational, what else could we look at too?

NOT What else could we do instead?

Feedback results in the person feeling motivated to change/grow/feel good

I found your performance to be outstanding. I also feel you have potential to be even better. Let's focus on a couple of areas you might be able to enhance even more.

NOT I think you can do better. What else can you do?

Feedback focuses on positive issues (for things done well) as well as the negative things to improve upon – always use a positive sandwich!

I think you're a great manager. I like how you have bonded with your team and they seem to be very inspired by you. Clara seems to need a bit of extra support as she tends to take a little longer to adjust than the others. What do you think you could do to inspire her a little more?

NOT You're not motivating Clara effectively.

When giving feedback the skill is to always:

1. First focus on the things someone did well,

2. Secondly then concentrate on the areas for improvement,

3. Finally end with something positive.

This format will always have a positive outcome and allows the coachee to feel motivated to change, not defensive or upset.

Self-fulfilling prophecy

Imagine this: What you focus on is what you get more of – the self-fulfilling prophecy.

So how could this work?

Well, when you ask someone to focus on their weak points or things that you'd see as negative, that just encourages negative feelings of lacking self-worth or guilt or, even worse, denial and rebellious behavior.

Imagine a child and telling them not to do something – isn't it highly likely that they will?

When you focus on the positive, and praise and encourage more of the same, that creates good feelings and more positivity which, in turn, results in more of the same.

describe the value before you ask for action effort to change.

To praise a child and encourage them for good behavior generally results in them wanting to please more, as they enjoy the recognition and praise.

I'm not saying ignore any areas for development but, simply see them as areas for development alongside areas of success. Focus on them in the proportion you use in a positive sandwich, i.e. 80 per cent positive with 20 per cent areas for development.

more positive than negative communication.

This strategy works with everyone – children, adults, employees and coachees.

A story of coaching

I read an article some time ago about an American sports coach who was viewed as the most successful sports coach in history because of how he managed and coached his football team.

The coach focused on what the players did right, not wrong. He inspired his players by videoing them and other players and taking time to show them how little adjustments to their stance could help their game. He only showed them the videos when they could correct their mistakes and see what they were doing right, never what they were doing wrong.

He also showed them videos of other players modeling exactly what he wanted so they could learn from them too.

He provided all the players with regular and positive feedback to reinforce progress instead of failure. He never wanted them to focus on what they were doing wrong or failure, only what they could do right and how to progress.

[handwritten note, left margin] Show the value benefit people can obtain not their mistakes

[handwritten note, bottom] Keep them working (constructive feedback).

[handwritten note, bottom] Showing value ⇒ bringing from their work positive feedback ⇒ to reinforce progress I never on what they are doing wrong failure

Skills practise

If you're working through this program alone you need to use every opportunity you can to practice all these skills. If you're working with someone else you'll need to work as partners and can use the following exercise. You can also adapt this for use in teaching communication styles to your team or department.

You need to practice:

✓ Building and establishing rapport

✓ Observing your own and others' body language

✓ Listening and questioning skills

✓ Summarizing skills

✓ Giving positive feedback

Exercise: Skills review

The aim is to review the skills learnt in this session.

With a partner, practice:

Building and establishing rapport

Observing your own and others' body language

Listening skills

Summarizing skills

Giving positive feedback

Person A

Talk for three minutes about a holiday you've had in the past

Person B

Practice:

Building and establishing rapport

Listening skills

Summarizing skills

Remember to establish and maintain rapport and be aware of how and where you sit – you should sit at an angle to the side (not facing) and as close as person A wishes. If you're unsure of the distance, ask them to place the chair where they want it. Remain aware of your and their body language.

It's active listening – don't take notes, just see how much you can remember. Don't interrupt or ask questions, just let person A talk and listen. If there's a silence, allow it.

After the three minutes, summarize to person A what you've heard and understood.

Person A

Practice giving positive feedback on person B's:

Rapport skills

Listening skills

Body language when coaching

Summarizing

Core coaching skills

NB: When receiving feedback, don't comment on or debate what you're hearing. Remain silent, listen to the feedback, accept it and thank the person. You'll probably be keen to comment, but remaining silent will allow you to feel how it is to receive feedback and not be able to or allowed to comment. Sometimes this is how people feel when receiving comments from their manager or supervisor.

Then switch and repeat the exercise so both of you practice all the skills.

Coaching corner

The value of positive feedback and modeling

The article I recalled is one of many success stories where coaches and great leaders have realized the value of this type of development. Focusing on someone's good points and encouraging them to continue and improve is very powerful as when a coachee/employee/co-worker/friend/partner or whoever feels respected, praised or even useful and appreciated they always want to do it more, that's our human nature and why children and adults respond to this kind of feedback in the same way.

The American coach also used something called 'modeling' which is something we cover in the next session and is all about focusing on skills or behaviors others do extremely well and finding a way to replicate it for yourself by studying their strategies. This is what the coach did with his players, focusing on what they did well plus what others did well and demonstrating, what to do, rather than, what not to do! Our brains all work to focus more on positive words rather than negative. So if you tell your coachee 'not to panic' when they do their next presentation their mind will skip the 'not to' bit and focus on panicking! A much better way to phrase it would be 'you may find it really easy to relax more next time you do a presentation' this way, they will be focusing on 'how easy it is to relax more' and panicking is not in their mind, as the words and thoughts were not highlighted.

transfer on others on possitive believes !!! ooo

Piracy

secret

Language and the way we use words is so important and makes such a huge difference. You may notice that your coachee uses a lot of negative words and phrases. It is essential to challenge them gently by explaining what impact these words have and how they are creating their own negative self-fulfilling prophecy.

Here are some tips on how to challenge a coachee with their language and how you can help them to rephrase their statements and break negative patterns:

Coachee: "I can't do it."

Coach: "You may not have it quite yet but you are learning fast."

Coachee: "I forget my words and panic when I see all their faces."

Coach: "It's interesting how people want you to succeed, when you see their faces willing you to do well it's easier to relax and remember all the things you can say to help them."

Coachee: "I want to go for the interview but I'm scared I won't be good enough or have the right experience."

Coach: "It's great that you want to try new experiences and it's interesting that you may very well have everything they are looking for and if you didn't get the job you would have still ensured that you gathered more experience by attending in the first place."

There are many more ways to re-phrase negative comments and also place a few encouraging statements in there too. Even if coachees reject what you are saying with a familiar 'yeah but' they will have still taken it on board and the little seed you planted will grow to challenge them later. You will be surprised how you can turn negativity into positivity quickly and easily by being aware of these language patterns.

seed positive perspective
(positive language & mind patterns).

Notes page

Personal reflection – Questioning and summarizing

Asking the right questions in the right way is a great skill to have and one that many people practice to get right. This is a skill coaches, sales people, managers, leaders and presenters all use but one which everyone would benefit from. Questions are as important as the positive phrases listed previously as often they also make a suggestion or imply something and generally communicate far more than you realize. Mastering good communication skills in using the right positive words and phrases, using good questions and being able to listen and summarize information succinctly are great life skills which will be of huge use anywhere and anytime. People will subconsciously judge you by your communication style and react to you based on that judgment. This will happen with a friend, co-worker, manager, staff member or even your partner.

Good questioning skills will also enable you to get people to reveal more relevant information. This questioning style is called 'chunking' and is something we cover in the next session.

I suggest you practice asking good open and closed questions as much as you can, at work, at home, in the supermarket and with strangers on the train, use anyone you can to practice with and notice the responses you get and how you can adapt and enhance your technique to get the information you want or need. Practice as often as you can so that when you learn about 'chunking' you will be ready to take your questioning skills to the next level.

Session 4

Coaching Strategies

"People will exceed targets they set themselves."

Gordon Dryden

Session 4

Coaching strategies

Objectives for session 4:

When you've practiced the ideas in this Session you should be able to:

✓ Use a variety of positive confidence-building techniques on yourself and others

✓ Describe how to create anchors and set them for yourself and others

✓ Recognize how people chunk information, and use the technique for clarity and information

✓ Describe the goal setting process in detail and show how it works

✓ Choose the coaching strategies that suit you best

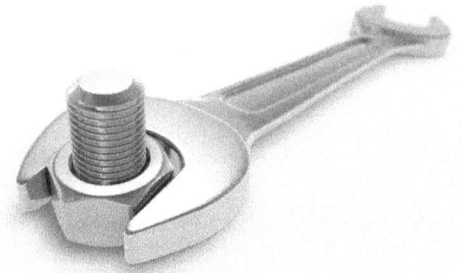

Tools in session 4:

- ✓ Modeling technique – used to learn skills, beliefs or behaviors from others who demonstrate them well.

- ✓ New behavior generator script – used to change patterns of behavior or negative beliefs.

- ✓ Anchoring script – used to create anchors/triggers to get into a positive belief or state using the senses.

- ✓ Pattern breaker techniques – used to interrupt coachees' negative belief or behavior patterns or to regain control of a session.

- ✓ Self coach exercise – for self reflection of your beliefs.

- ✓ Letter of commitment – used to document achievements over a 12 month period for focus and determination to succeed.

- ✓ Letter of positivity – group exercise used to build confidence and inspire/motivate/challenge limiting beliefs of self.

- ✓ Relaxation technique – used any time to relax and induce calm for clarity and focus.

- ✓ Chunking – questioning technique used to get more or less information from the coachee – advanced questioning techniques. This can also be used for conflict resolution.

- ✓ Sun diagrams – for ideas of how to achieve goals/issues.

- ✓ Well formed outcome – used to clarify if goals are worth pursuing/achieving as some may have negative outcomes.

✓ Goal setting criteria – guidelines of what to cover when setting goals

✓ 5-Step goal setting model – used for goal setting

✓ STEPPPA model – used for goal setting

✓ TGROW model – used for goal setting

So far during this program we've looked at a lot of theory and given you some solid background to effective coaching. We're now getting into the practicalities more, focusing on the coaching models, tools you can use to start to set goals, change behaviors, work with conflict, reframe viewpoints and monitor and evaluate progress.

This is your tool bag of coaching strategies. We provide you with many so you can choose the ones that suit you and others best. Remember, one strategy doesn't fit all. We all have different learning styles, beliefs, behaviors and personality types as we saw in Session 2, so you can pick and choose which best fit the person and the situation.

Modeling

If you could choose someone to be like ...

Someone you really admire and would want to be ...

Someone who has skills you want or behaves in a way you aspire to be ...

... Who would it be?

build scale of your dream (dream big in being now)

Modeling is an NLP method of development and is focused on modeling the skills and excellence of people. By noticing what they do and noticing what works, you can then design useful models and processes that enable you to make changes in yourself quickly, to install the excellence you want (like the coach did with the exemplars he filmed to show his players as discussed in Session 3).

By learning to recognize patterns and create new ones, you can successfully replicate any excellent behavior or skill you see in others.

If you want to acquire a skill or adopt a new behavior, or even adapt a current behavior, find someone who does it better than you, or does it exactly as you would like to do it, and model them – i.e. copy what they do.

Often, you don't have to re-invent the wheel. There's always someone, somewhere, who can do or has conquered the same area you wish to change. All you need to do is find out EXACTLY how they do or did it and do EXACTLY the same.

Modeling is used a lot with sports coaching, and can be used in any area of life with any behavior or situation.

Exercise:

Think about a behavior you'd like to create or change.

For example, how you could be more confident in interviews, meetings or general life. Now think about someone you know who already does this easily and effortlessly. You can model them and learn the skill of supreme confidence – if they can do it, so can you!

It doesn't have to be someone you know, it can be someone you know of, even a famous person or someone who has died. You just need to either imagine how they did it if you have some knowledge of them or truly research and study them for exact fine detail.

Select someone now and write below why you picked them and what you would like to model. Then go through the following script, new behavior generator, to learn how to model someone. *(Leonardo da Vinci) ?*

Tesla, Benjamin Franklin, Mick Jagger ⇒ creativity/innovation

Warren Buffet, Jozef Beros, Google, Jack Ma, Napoleon, Hitler Stalin (think big)

Steve Jobs, Roccefeler, Beros, Buffet (?)
— they didn't value money, they valued their job.

[margin notes:]
imagination think big
idea and money in my life
(till now is too mistreated

New behavior generator

The New-Behavior Generator helps people change a behavior or habit they already have, or helps them to acquire a new behavior or skill they want to have.

Read through the following script to understand the process. We suggest you use this exactly as it is with willing volunteers to practice your skills; then you can use it with your coachees.

Remember:

✓ Establish rapport before you begin.

✓ Get the coachee to close their eyes and relax so they feel comfortable doing this (asking them to take a few deep breaths and sit comfortably will help too).

✓ Leave gaps in the script where the coachee may need to think or visualize things.

✓ Follow the script.

IMPORTANT

New behavior generator script

1. Pick a behavior or skill you'd like to have in a particular situation. It can be something you've experienced or a situation you've never been in before (e.g., being confident in an interview or at a specific event). *reaching for money (in order to be rich).*

2. Select a model – a real or imaginary person. It can also be someone who's died if you wish. Someone who elegantly and effortlessly exhibits this behavior or skill. *Buffet, Jobs request, take effort to master finances.*

3. Make a movie. You're the director watching your model perform this behavior or skill in the situation you want to use it.
   See the images and hear the sounds of the model as he or she goes through the situation you've picked. If you're not satisfied at this point, pick a different model until you are satisfied and everything is as you want it.

4. Now run the movie from start to finish, seeing them doing whatever it is exactly as you see it. Watch them closely, paying attention to their movements, language, actions and reactions, beliefs and expectations of the situation.
   See what they see, hear what they hear, feel what they feel, just as you would whilst watching a movie. The movie can move at any pace.
   Let me know when you've finished by nodding your head.
   <Wait for them to let you know before continuing>

5. Ok, now you've finished, run the movie again, and this time add yourself to it, mimicking them exactly.
   You can be beside them or behind them, imitating and copying their actions, movements, body language, words, tone of voice – everything.

6. Notice the responses your model is getting from those around them. Notice how it feels to receive those same responses yourself. See what you see, feel what you feel and hear what you hear as you watch, listen and mimic your model.
   Notice any finer distinctions you need to make and adjust for yourself to be copying them exactly and make those changes.

Let me know when you're ready to continue by nodding your head.
<Wait for them to let you know before continuing>

7. Now, imagine climbing inside your model, becoming one and the same.
Notice how the model now becomes you. See yourself there instead of them – your own image, voice and soundtrack.
Is it all ok? If not, make a few adjustments until it is.
As you look through what were their eyes in the same movie, consider how this new behavior will affect your life and those around you. Is it an appropriate healthy behavior to have for your benefit and those around you? If not make any necessary changes to modify the behavior. If you're happy that it's good and as you thought, then continue, let me know when you are ready.
<Wait for them to let you know before continuing>

8. While still inside the image, run the movie again with you doing the same things they did in exactly the same way.
Feel what it's like to be like this and to have this new behavior as a normal effortless behavior for you.
Enhance the feeling and make it stronger, notice what you see, feel and hear in detail as you run the movie. Nod when you're ready.
<Wait for them to let you know before continuing>

9. Now run the movie again. Feel what it's like to be in your own body having this new behavior.
See all around you how other people and other things look and how others respond to you when you have this new behavior.
What new things are you telling yourself? How differently does your future look? How differently do you look at your past? What new wonderful feelings do you have as a result of having this new behavior? <Pause>

10. Ask yourself, when would be a good time to use this new behavior in the near future? What will you see, hear and feel that indicates to you that it would be useful to begin to behave in this new fashion?

<Pause>
Really live it, visualize it and make it real.

11. Just step to the side for a second, as a producer again, and just see if you need to make any final adjustments or if it's exactly how you want it.
   If you need to tweak it, do so now and then step back into it. Step back into it at the end of the movie, look back and remember what it was like to exhibit that new behavior. See what you saw, feel what you felt, hear what you heard. Learn what you need to learn. Take all the time you need to take in those new learnings. <Pause>

12. When you've finished, take a moment to feel proud of the work you've done. Open your eyes when you're ready.

<End script>   ఴ I LOVE IT

You may need to repeat this process a couple of times if they struggled to get it all the first time.

This exercise is good for people who can visualize easily. If someone finds it hard to visualize, another strategy may be more effective. This strategy is generally very effective and can encourage quick and rapid change. It's also a tool the coachee can repeat themselves once they know the steps to take.

Tips:

Get your partner to select their model or models before the exercise as it can sometimes take a while for them to choose.

If someone says they can't visualize, get them to answer these two questions;
Can you remember what a grey elephant looks like?
Can you imagine what a pink elephant with two trunks would look like?

If they can do both they can remember images and create images, therefore they can visualize as the second question involves visualizing.

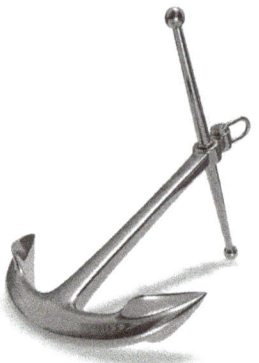

Anchors and pattern breakers/interrupts

The term 'anchoring' and 'setting anchors' may be new to you but the process of anchors won't be, as you've been practicing them without knowing all of your life.

If you've got a favorite song you play and it makes you feel good because it reminds you of the great holiday you had last year then that's an anchor. Maybe you smell fish and chips and feel calm and comfortable because you always used to have them when you relaxed on a Friday night after a long week at work. It might be that if you put on your favorite suit and it makes you feel special as you only wear it for great occasions. Then you've already experienced anchors!

Anchors aren't always about connecting to good feelings, perhaps the smell of whisky makes you instantly feel sick because you drank way too much several years ago and were dreadfully ill or hearing a certain song makes you feel sad because it reminds you of a lost love.
These are all anchors and triggers: external stimuli automatically setting off internal changes.

> Anchoring is the process by which a memory, an emotion or another response is associated with something else.
> When that something else occurs, the original inner state is triggered, and you experience it again.

By deliberately associating a specific experience to a stimulus, you can trigger the experience whenever you want and feel the way you want to, whenever you need to. You can use all your senses when creating anchors, and it can happen consciously or unconsciously. (Just think of some of the previous examples!).

Anchors link us to feelings, good or bad, which in NLP (neuro linguistic programming) are called 'states'. States can be changed at any time and coachees can learn how to do this at will to help them to get out of negative states or into a positive state.

Old negative anchors can be changed or 'collapsed' and new positive anchors programed in to replace them.
Anchors are highly effective at changing feelings and moods within seconds and are an easy to adopt tool for change.

Work through the following script to learn how to set anchors for yourself and others.

Anchoring states can be done using:

➢ Touch

➢ Smell

➢ Taste

➢ Sight

➢ Sound

By using a combination of the senses you can enhance the anchor and make it stronger, so feel free to experiment.

To anchor a resourceful state:

Build rapport – ask the coachee to get comfortable however they wish. Sit or stand close by but to the side (not head on) and ask them what emotion (state) they want to anchor and where they would like to anchor to on their body.

Help them to access the state – ask them to think about a time they felt that way or see how it feels to be like that. Keep asking them questions to build the feeling so it gets more intense. They can also add to it by describing other times they had this feeling. Let them think and visualize and gently assist with open questions about the feeling if they get stuck.

Tell them to see what they saw, feel what they felt and hear what they heard.

Anchor the state – when they're in the feeling they want to achieve. You'll know this by their body language and from what they say. Ask them to set their anchor, to pinch, squeeze, press or hold whichever part of their hand, arm, ear or leg etc they've chosen, and continue to do this as they feel the maximum strength of the desired feeling.

Test the state – when you feel the state is anchored, ask them to open their eyes, tell you their telephone number backwards (to break the state) and then ask them to test the anchor by doing the action they chose.

If they get the feeling the anchor has worked, they can then build on this anchor to strengthen it by repeating the process and adding new events to it as they go along.

If they don't feel the state, repeat the process.

The script that follows takes people through the anchoring process.

Anchoring script

> **Remember:**
>
> ✓ Establish rapport before you begin.
>
> ✓ Get the coachee to close their eyes and relax so they feel comfortable doing this (asking them to take a few deep breaths and sit comfortably will help too).
>
> ✓ Leave gaps in between the script where the coachee may need to think or visualize things.
>
> ✓ Follow the script.

Anchoring script

1. Pick a behavior or skill you'd like to have in a particular situation. It can be something you've experienced, or a situation you've never been in before (e.g., being confident in an interview or a specific event).

2. Now decide how you'd like to anchor this behavior or skill in your body using touch. You could pinch your thumb and index finger together, make a fist, squeeze your knee, pinch your ear, squeeze your wrist or anything you wish. Choose something you can do any time to trigger your anchor.

3. You don't need to give me any details throughout this exercise other than how you intend to set your anchor and what behavior or feeling you wish to anchor.
    <For the purpose of this script we're assuming it will be anchored by squeezing their fist and that the feeling is confidence – you'll need to change the details for your coachees.>

4. So, can you tell me now how you wish to set your anchor?
    <Answer: 'Squeezing the fist of my right hand'>

5. Can you also tell me what behavior or feeling you wish to anchor?
    <Answer: 'Confidence'>

6. Now, I'd like you to close your eyes and imagine what it would be like to feel incredibly confident.
    <For other feelings just replace the word 'confident' with the feeling/skill/emotion they've chosen>

7. Remember a time in your life when you felt confident.

8. If you can't remember a time when you were confident, remember a time when you saw someone else feeling supremely confident and imagine what it would feel like to be them.

9. Really focus on how it feels to be confident and allow that feeling to grow.

10. How does confidence taste?

11. What color is confidence?

12. Stand or sit as a confident person would.

13. Really feel what confidence feels like – allow that feeling to build now, make it more intense.

14. What would confidence sound like, if it had a sound?

15. Remember another time when you were fabulously confident in your life or when you felt really good.

16. Imagine a time when you will be really confident and how that will feel.

17. Now take that feeling of supreme confidence, add in any colors, smell, taste and sound and make that confident feeling grow stronger and stronger, almost like an energy that starts to vibrate with great strength, see it getting bigger and bigger.

18. Imagine a dial in front of you, like a volume dial on a music system with a maximum of ten. Reach forward and take hold of that dial. Start to turn it up towards ten. As you do, see the confidence in you growing more and more.

19. Turn that dial all the way up to maximum and as you do, feel the confidence at top strength and intensity, buzzing and vibrating with tremendous energy.

20. When you feel it at its peak, I want you to make a fist with your right hand and squeeze firmly. Either hold the squeeze or release and repeat it a few times whilst the intensity of the feeling of confidence continues. That's right <Say this as you observe them doing this.>

21. When you're ready, I want you to open your eyes.

22. Okay, what's your telephone number backwards? <This will break their state>

23. Now, <or whatever action they have decided to use to set the anchor> make a fist with your right hand and tell me how you feel. <To test the anchor worked>

24. Now, whenever you need to feel confident, all you need to do is make a fist with your right hand. You'll need to practice this and make the anchor really strong. From now on, any time you feel really good or confident make a fist in the same way.

<End script>

If they feel confidence, even slight confidence, then it has worked. If they feel nothing you need to repeat the exercise.

Tips:

The coachee must continue to strengthen the anchor so that the positive emotion is stronger than the negative ones it's going to replace. If it's not strong enough, there's a risk that when they trigger the anchor (when they make a fist) the stronger negative emotions could be anchored instead. Then, when they trigger that anchor in future it will make them feel the negative emotion. This will not happen if they practice and strengthen the anchor you set with them.

Pattern breakers

Sometimes during a coaching session, a coachee can become distressed and go into an emotional state, becoming either upset or angry, and go into a rant or get engrossed with wanting to tell you the story in complete detail. They start to feel the feelings they associate with the situation they're describing. But this isn't required in coaching, as past events and painful times are more to do with therapy.

When this happens, it's important to remove the coachee from this state so that the coaching session can proceed.

Breaking a person's state is called a pattern break or interrupt. It can also be used when people go into an old behavior pattern and get stuck in their response like a broken record, doing the same thing over and over. Pattern breakers are effective at interrupting these behaviors and quickly changing the coachee's states.

A pattern break can be anything from sneezing, dropping something on the floor, swatting an imaginary fly or pretending to see something out of the window. Anything you can think of to gently and politely interrupt the coachee's train of thought.

You can also ask them random questions which will confuse the brain or break their flow, such as 'what's your telephone number backwards?', 'what did you have for dinner last night?', 'what color is your front door?' (These are more obvious pattern interrupts and you can explain to the coachee your reason for using them, if you want.)

Once they stop talking, you quickly change the subject and bring the session back on track.

The more you can help to break a pattern of a rant or 'victim mentality/poor me' type of conversation, the more you'll help the coachee to focus on making positive changes and not revisiting negative feelings over and over.

Note:

If the coachee is suffering with emotional trauma, pattern interrupts may not be appropriate. Remember, you can refer a coachee to a professional therapist or coach if you feel it's relevant as you might do more harm than good, working outside of your capabilities.

[Creating new good patern is important]

not reflecting on emotions or give freedom to subject.

we guide person, limiting his freedom to expression.

Confidence building techniques

Exercise: Self-Coaching

Do you believe you're a confident person?

Do you believe you're not a confident person?

Whichever you believe is true.

We create our own reality based on our beliefs of ourselves and others. Changing negative or limiting beliefs into positive beliefs can have life-changing effects.

Beliefs questionnaire:

Answer the following questions (there are no right or wrong answers, just write your first response with whatever words come to mind).

How do you see yourself?

....

....

....

....

What do you believe about yourself?
(Make a list of whatever comes to mind.)

How do you think others see you?

How would you like them to think about you?

Consider this: What you wrote – what you believe –
creates your reality and is how it will be.

If that's the case, what do you want to write/believe?

You don't need to believe what you write right now. You took time to create your negative beliefs (which may not have even been yours and suggested or given to you by someone from your past, such as a teacher, parent, child in the school playground, ex-partner, etc). So it might take time to adopt new ones.

All you need to do is:

✓ Decide what you want to believe instead

✓ Write it/them down

✓ Look at it/them daily

✓ Start to live as if you are already like that. You soon will be, because you get what you focus on – trust me!

Exercise: Coachee/group coaching

Ask your coachee or each member of the group to do the following:

Write five statements of confidence or affirmations (positive belief statements) that you believe or want to believe about yourself.

State these beliefs with conviction in front of the group or coach – do they believe you?

The group or coach will give feedback on how convincing you are – you need to convince them it is true and really feel it.

All group members list other members' beliefs to create a comprehensive list of positive beliefs and affirmations they can all focus on or the coach and coachee can more together.

Some examples of positive affirmations:

- ➢ I am a confident and capable person.
- ➢ My confidence grows daily.
- ➢ I am positive and focused to achieve my goals.
- ➢ I achieve easily and effortlessly.
- ➢ I learn and grow every day.
- ➢ I believe in myself, I can achieve anything I want to.

Exercise: Letter of commitment – self-coach

Consider what you want to achieve and your commitment to change the things you've identified and how that change will enhance your life.

Include goals you'll achieve within the next 12 months (these will be covered later in this session, so you might want to complete those exercises first).

Now write a letter to yourself as if you've already achieved them. Describe how you feel, how your life has changed and all the benefits and rewards you're enjoying from those changes.

Who is in your life who wasn't before? Who's no longer in your life? How are you financially? How is your health? What are you doing now? What are your hobbies? Where do you live? What do you now believe? How do you spend your days? What do you contribute? How grateful do you feel for what you have now and how your life has become?

Write about how proud of yourself you are and how great life is.

Put that letter with your goal setting documents and beliefs list in your diary or on your wall. Somewhere you can see it and review it daily. This is your commitment to change and your motivation – you can and will have what you've written if you want it and are prepared to go and get it.

---

ciekawe

Exercise: Letter of positivity – group coach

This is a wonderful exercise to do with a group as it leaves everyone with something they can refer back to that will always make them smile and feel good. It is also something that you could get friends and family to create for you if you are working through this alone. If working with friends or family you could just ask them to write comments for you and then collate them.

Each take a piece of A4 paper and write your name on the top.

Pass the paper to the person to your right.

Write something good, a compliment or an observation about the person whose name is the top of the paper. It can be about them physically such as 'has beautiful eyes/nice smile/lovely hair/pretty face/great figure' or it could be about their personality, such as 'always makes me laugh/supports me/cheers me up/helps people'.

When you've written the comment, fold the paper over so the next person can only see the name at the top and pass it on.

Continue until you get your piece of paper back, i.e., it's gone around the whole group

Fold your paper, put it somewhere safe and read it later or the next day. Don't try to analyze who wrote what – it doesn't matter. Just enjoy the compliments and feel good.

Pin it on your fridge or somewhere you can read it regularly to feel good in an instant!

Say something good about yourself. ☺
daily exercise

Relaxation technique for calm and focus

Sometimes, all that's required is to just relax, to feel good and clear your mind. Here is a simple relaxation technique you can do for yourself or use to help others. Doing this each night before you go to sleep will help you to let go of the day's activities and get a sound night's sleep. It can also be used to prepare yourself for meditation, or relax during the day should you need to, and is great to help with stress and anxiety.

Relaxation script:

1. Sit upright or lie down and get as comfortable as you can with your arms in an open posture, or on your thighs or chair arms. Uncross your legs and have your feet flat on the floor if sitting. Remove your shoes if you wish.

2. Close your eyes and begin to focus on your breath.
    Take three deep breaths from the abdomen and try to remain focused on the breath, allowing any thoughts to leave your mind.
    Zone out from any distractions or noise by bringing your focus and attention back to the breath.

3. Take your awareness to your feet and notice any tension present.
    Allow the tension to be released.
    Let the muscles in your feet go and let your feet feel heavy, as if they were sinking into the ground.

4. Now take your awareness to your ankles, calves, the front of your legs and all the way up to your knee sockets.
   Scan for any tension and let it go, allowing it to flow down your legs and out of the end of your toes.
   Remember to breathe, breathing in relaxation and allowing the breath to breathe out tension and anything you don't need.

5. Take your awareness to your upper legs and hips.
   Scan for any tension and let it go, allowing it to flow down your legs and out of the end of your toes.

6. Now move up to your stomach and lower back, up to your chest and upper back.
   Scan for any tension and let it go, allowing it to flow down your body, all the way down and out through the end of your toes.
   Breathing in deep relaxation and calm, and breathing out stress and tension.

7. Take your attention to your shoulders, upper arms, elbows and down through your lower arms.
   Allowing any tension you find to gently flow down your arms and be released through the ends of your fingers.
   Feeling more deeply relaxed and calm now.

8. Focus on the back of your neck, up the back of your head, top of your head to your forehead, eyebrows, eyes, behind your eyes, cheekbones, ears, tip of your nose, lips and chin
   Allow any tension to flow away down and out of your body.
   The breath bringing total calm and relaxation and removing any last bits of remaining tension from your whole body.
   Your whole body now feels heavy and relaxed, fully supported by the chair or bed.

9. Imagine a beam of light entering the top of your head and gently scanning down your body for any tiny remnants of tension and dissolving them as it flows through.
   It's a color that you like or that means something to you.
   When it reaches your feet, it changes to a color of great healing and calm and starts an upward flow, filling your body, repairing and renewing anything that needs it as it goes along.
   When it reaches the top of your head, the color stays within your body.

10. There is nothing for you to do, only relax and focus on your breath.
    Continue to breathe and focus on the color you have chosen.
    Relax here for as long as you like.

11. When you're ready to move, gently wiggle your fingers and toes and slowly open your eyes.
    Allow yourself to come back to full consciousness slowly and have a good stretch before you stand up and continue with your day.

If you carry out this exercise regularly, you'll find it will refresh you and help you cope with the pressures and demands of life. The more you do it, the easier it will be and the quicker you'll be able to reach a deep level of relaxation.

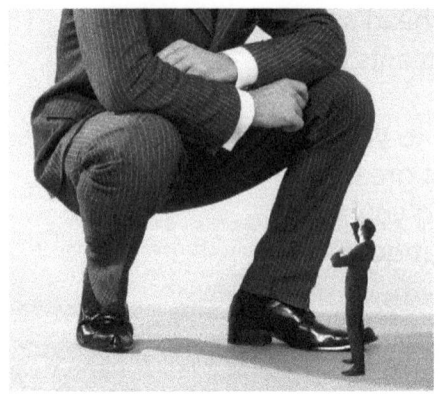

Chunking

Chunking is a brilliant technique to use when trying to get more information from a coachee or to work with them to resolve conflict.

Everyone chunks information in different sizes and some people are naturally large chunkers and other small.

A person can chunk upwards, downwards or sideways.

A large chunker if asked what they do for a job might say 'I'm a teacher'.

A small chunker might say 'I'm an English teacher for children with learning difficulties, aged 5 to 11, at a center down the road'.

Large chunkers - the big picture

If you're coaching a large chunker, you'll have to encourage them to chunk down by asking questions to get more information.

Large chunkers just need to grasp the point, the general direction only and can't abide the steps, specifics and details unless they have a point. Even then, they prefer to delegate the details.

These are big picture thinkers, dreamers and direction setters.

Small chunkers - the details

Small chunkers need the details, specifics, the concrete steps, and without that, they see a goal as a dream or pie in the sky. They prefer to work out all the steps on the way.

If you have a small chunker you might encourage them to chunk up, as they'll take too long to give you information and you might not need it in such detail.

Large and small chunkers drive each other crazy because they are so different and extreme from each other in the way they think and act, yet both types are necessary in the workplace and general life. Most people are somewhere in the middle but will have traits towards one style.

Chunking and Conflict Resolution

When resolving conflict between people or departments, chunking is an excellent tool to use to get everyone working towards and agreeing with one common goal. You'll need to get everyone to chunk up until they all reach the same chunk.

Here's an example: Say you have one person who's complaining about the speed of another department's paperwork and its delivery to them, and the other department complaining about the amount of paperwork they have to complete and the time it takes.

Chunking down would go into their individual issues and problems in more depth causing further conflict and a probable stalemate.

So, chunk up – ask them to consider what the paperwork is for. The answer will be something like 'to give us information for the patient/coachee/customer'.

Then chunk up again – ask about the patient/coachee/customer. And you might get the answer that they're here to help patients/

coachees/customers, and they both agree that is their common role.

Now chunk back down – ask for solutions, encouraging them to work together to resolve the amount of paperwork and the time it takes to complete with the shared goal of helping the patient/coachee/customer. They are now working together with a common goal and not against each other in conflict.

Example of chunking down

Wardrobe – brown wardrobe – large brown wardrobe – large brown oak wardrobe. (More detail as goes down)

Example of chunking up

Double bed – bed – furniture – object (Less detail as goes up)

Example of sideways chunking

Car-van-truck-motorbike-train (all modes of transport)

Suggested chunking questions

To encourage a coachee to chunk up, ask questions such as:
➢ What is this an example of?
➢ What is the bigger picture?
➢ What's the bigger issue here?
➢ For what purpose?
➢ What is your higher intention?
➢ What will having that give you?

Chunking down questions would be:
➢ What's an example of this?
➢ What's a specific example?
➢ When specifically did this occur?
➢ What are the pieces that make this thing up?
➢ What can I break this down into?
➢ What was a specific example or specific time?
➢ What are the steps or details?

Example of sideways chunking:
➢ What's another example of this?
➢ What's another example of the same thing?
➢ What else do you dislike?
➢ What else?

Goal setting and
goal criteria

Once choices have been explored, you can help the coachee go through the choices and identify a goal or goals. Exploration covers any steps to the goal that might be necessary, so you'll need to check with them that it is achievable (viable), that they're fully motivated to begin and they have an established action plan that includes time-scales for each step.

When the coachee identifies a goal they want to achieve, it's important that they follow a set process to ensure all the goal setting criteria are there and covered. If the goal is a large goal it should be broken down into smaller, more easily achievable steps to ensure the coachee experiences successes along the way and doesn't become frustrated.

There are many different ways to establish goal setting criteria, including the NLP concept of well formed outcomes. Other coaching strategies are SMART, STEPPPA, PROGRAM, GROW and TGROW models (we discuss some of these later in the session).

Sun diagrams

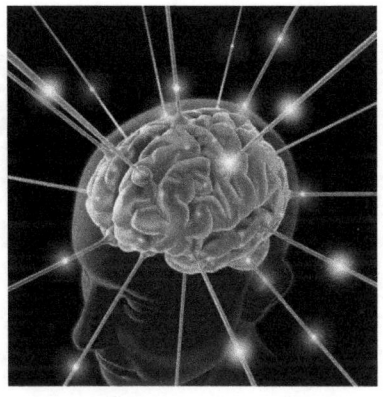

You need to encourage your coachee to find many options and ways to achieve goals, so that they get many routes to the same outcome. If your coachee is struggling to come up with solutions to attain their goal, or if they need to look at alternative options to achieve that goal, a sun diagram is a useful tool.

When you create a sun diagram (or mini-mindmap) you focus on one issue at a time. You then brainstorm, looking at all possibilities or suggestions. In true brainstorming-style you write down everything at first – however whacky it might seem.

You can then decide which of the options are viable and go through the goal setting criteria. We take you through the process in detail in Session 5. First, here's an example of a sun diagram for a very specific goal.

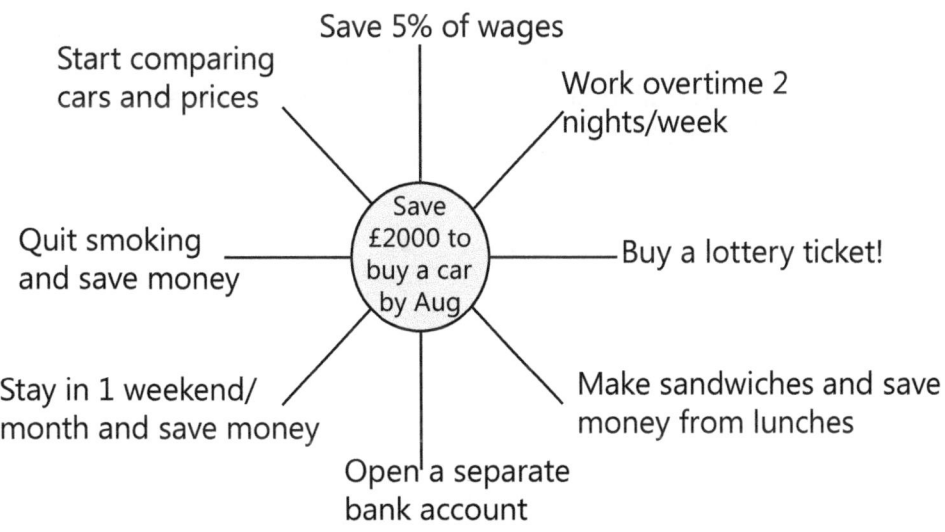

Well formed outcomes

It's important to check that the goals you've chosen are right for you in every way. Some people select goals they think are good for them without realizing they might have to give things up or make sacrifices to achieve them. If they knew, they'd probably rather not aim for that goal and would prefer to choose another.

For example, if you wanted to be a millionaire: it sounds really good, but have you considered how much extra time you'd have to work, perhaps doing more than one job? Or how much you'd need to focus on saving rather than spending money on social activities or holidays? Or that the time working extra hours might have a negative impact on your relationship with children, family and friends?

Don't just rush off with what seems like a great goal – check every one first and make sure it's a goal you really want to achieve.

We take you through the process of creating a well formed outcome in detail in Session 5. But to give you a feel for it, here's the checklist we'll use:

Exercise: Well formed outcome checklist

State the goal or desired outcome positively.

- ❏ Is it specific or could you define it more, is it measurable?
- ❏ Can you achieve it by yourself?
- ❏ Is the goal positive and ethical to benefit you or others around you i.e. does it have a positive intention?
- ❏ How will you know when you have it? How will you feel?
- ❏ Why don't you have it now? Has anything stopped you?
- ❏ How big a goal is it? Do you need to break it up into smaller goals?
- ❏ What are all the steps you need to take?
- ❏ When will you take the first step?
- ❏ When will you complete it all?
- ❏ Are there any other ways to get it?
- ❏ What resources do you currently have (physical, emotional, mental, spiritual, financial, knowledge, skills, assistance etc)?
- ❏ What resources will you need?
- ❏ What will you need to give up to have it? How will it affect you (friends, work, relationships, lifestyle etc)?
- ❏ What will happen if you don't get it? How will you feel?
- ❏ What will happen if you do get it? How will you feel?
- ❏ If you don't get it, will you lose out on anything?
- ❏ If you do get it, will you lose out anything?
- ❏ What will having it give to you? For what purpose do you want it?
- ❏ Will achieving this goal enhance your life and others'?
- ❏ Is it a worthwhile goal to aim to achieve?
- ❏ Do you still want to achieve this goal?

Goal setting criteria

When setting goals, it's important to follow these criteria:

➢ Have target dates by which you will achieve them – be specific with dates.

➢ Review them daily – put them in your diary or on your wall and read each day.

➢ Make sure they're clearly defined – that they're specific and detailed.

➢ Have a means of measuring progress towards achievement – you can assess whether you are achieving or moving towards achieving them or not.

➢ Choose a reward for every goal, to be enjoyed when achieved – the reward can be anything and it doesn't necessarily have to cost any money.

➢ Be set without limits, no matter how large – dream big, choose anything you want.

➢ Break goals into smaller steps if necessary – if it's a large goal, make it into smaller stages which when achieved make up the achievement of the large goal.

➢ Have a defined support infrastructure – ask for help, you don't have to do it all by yourself!

Goal setting sheet example

This is how to make sure you cover all the criteria in the list.

A blank version can be downloaded from the website www.UoLearn.com.

Goal	Get promoted to senior leader	Improve my management skills
Action points	Research the post Speak to my manager Apply for the position Practice interview skills Get a new suit	Finish coaching course Ask Peter to mentor me Team building exercise Ask for feedback from my team
Why and what benefit	Happier, more money, better hours, challenge	Better manager Happier with myself and work Less stressed
Who can help and how	Manager Partner Colleagues	Supervisor Leadership course Personal coach
Date to be achieved	1st April	31st April
Results and actions so far + / -	Applied for job No success meeting with manager	Been on stress management course in Feb
Date actually achieved	30th May	28th April
Reward	Celebrate by going out for a family meal	Book a weekend break
Advice for next time	Need more to time to achieve all points i.e. took longer than I expected.	Believe in myself because I proved that I can do it!

Goal setting models

Below are two other goal setting methods you can use for yourself or with others.

In Session 5 we'll show you how to use them with a coachee.

STEPPPA model

S Subject (issue)

T Target objective, if already known

E Emotional context (subject and target) to gain motivation

P Perception made consciously for new choices
(target re-evaluation)

P Plan: procedure of the STEPs leading to the target

P Pace: checking the plan for realism, team-fit and consequences

A Adapt or Action the Plan

Subject

This will be the content of the session i.e. the topic/issue being discussed. It might be the topic for a whole coaching session or just one small part of it. It could be a collection of issues to turn into goals or one goal and it is from this that the target (goal) is chosen.

Target

The target will be the actual goal or goals and will need to be clearly defined. If the coachee has one or more goals, the coach will need to ask some specific questions to clarify they have clear ideas of how to set and achieve the goal/goals they are setting.

Emotion

The coach will need to check that the motivation and emotional commitment is there to achieve the target or goal. Do they really want it? Do they prioritize it as high on their agenda? Are they committed enough to achieve it? Asking them how committed they are to achieving the goal on a scale of 0 to 10 (10 fully committed, 0 no commitment at all) is a good way to gauge this. For example if a coachee replies five they are not going to invest time and effort to achieve it, if they state ten then they are fully committed.

Perception

The aim is to encourage conscious perception and a number of potential, achievable choices for going forward and achieving the goal. The coach will encourage the coachee to look at various ways of achieving the goal, to consider areas they may not have considered and to look at all avenues and options. The coach will also challenge the coachee to consider different ways of thinking and also be able to work with any behaviors and beliefs which may help or hinder the process.

Plan

The plan is the way forward to achieve the goal and the actions required to do this. If the coachee is confused at this point and still considering lots of options without selecting a clear path then they are not ready to move forward and more discussion and thought is required. More perceptual work will then be necessary, including assessing the pros and cons of each choice, in order to get fixed on one plan.

Pace

This will finalize the goal setting stage by introducing the time frames and ensuring that they are realistic and achievable. Does the pace fit with other priorities including work, home and social demands? It is important to set specific deadlines to achieve any goal but it doesn't have to be set in stone and time scales can move from time to time. Coachees will become more accurate as they learn about themselves and how well they predict their time frames. Whilst setting time frames is an important and crucial part of effective goal setting it is okay to change them along the way if required.

Adapt or Action

The coach should seek information that shows a commitment to achievable timescales and challenge this as necessary. If inadequate, then further work is needed to check commitment and explore what, if anything, stops them or is required to help them to achieve their goal. Otherwise the plan is put into action and monitored.

TGROW model

T Theme (initial understanding)

G Goal

R Reality (who/what/where/how much?)

O Options (what's possible?)

W Will or Wrap Up (clarity/commitment and support)

Theme
The theme of the session.

Goal
The coachee defines the one clear goal they want to work on.
They then state the outcome they want and by when they intend
to achieve it. It might be broken down into smaller steps and
time scales if required. The coach works with the coachee to
establish a clear, measurable, specific goal.

Reality
The coach helps the coachee to understand all the factors
impacting on the goal that could hinder its achievement
or progress. This will include working with any beliefs and
behaviors which could be a barrier to the success of achieving
their goal and reinforcing positive beliefs which will assist to
ensure it is achieved.

belief I have to be prepared

Options
Options are explored by coach and coachee. Mind Mapping
is very useful at this stage. All options are considered and the
coachee will make their own choices of how to move forward.

Will
Once the coachee has chosen their way forward, i.e. what
actions to take to achieve their clear goal, they are able to
consider making this into a plan. All areas are considered
including time frames, specific actions, other involved,
motivation and determination to succeed, level of commitment,
ways of monitoring and evaluating the success and rewards
when achieved.

Monitoring, evaluating, reviewing and developing

An effective coach will ensure the coachee is accountable and motivated to work towards the goal. Regular meetings, phone calls or email contact supporting the coachee and encouraging them to stay positive and working towards the goal are necessary.

Sometimes goals may not be achieved or timescales missed.

This is perfectly okay and you should make sure your coachee doesn't feel downhearted about this. Goals can be changed, discarded, added to and timescales extended if necessary. A goal should never cause unhealthy pressure or distress and sometimes things change. The coachee should be encouraged to adapt and understand change whilst maintaining their motivation and drive to succeed.

As one goal or step is achieved, new ones will grow and develop, as it's a process of growth and development.

Coachees should be encouraged to use the goal setting process and criteria for all areas of their life and to make short-term monthly goals as well as mid-term (1 year) goals and long-term (3–5 or 10+ year) goals.

Coachees can determine what a short, mid and long term goal is to them and then form a desired path to follow and achieve the life they want to live.

If a coachee is unsure of the areas to goal-set for, they can use the Life Areas Assessment which you completed in Session 1 – this will give them focus for their priorities and is a good starting point.

It's also a good tool to use to evaluate 3 to 6 months after goals have been set, to see if any change has occurred for the coachee which could be positive or negative; and then again three to six months later as an ongoing measurement tool.

Coaching corner

Setting anchors

We touch on anchoring during this program and use an example and script of how to help a coachee to build self confidence. It is important to note that although we focus on creating positive anchors, some coachees may have unknowingly created negative anchors for themselves which have been practiced and well rehearsed over the years. For example if someone puts their fingers on their mouth, bites their nails, stands in a certain position, clenches their hands, taps their feet etc. they are using the same senses such as touch that we focus on yet in this case unknowingly to create their own negative anchors. When they repeat these movements they will get the same feeling they were trying to avoid, i.e. feeling nervous. When they are nervous they will unconsciously perform these movements which further reinforces the feeling or 'state'.

These are called negative anchors and sometimes it is necessary to highlight them to the coachee before moving to create positive ones. As we discussed during the section on anchoring, if a positive anchor is not reinforced and practiced it will not be strong and when an anchor is being set the strongest emotion will be anchored, if this is negative such as worry, nervousness, anxiety etc then this will become the anchor rather than confidence or whatever the coachee is trying to achieve. It is generally quite simple to spot or discover any negative anchors by observing the coachee's body language and identifying what they demonstrate physically and verbally (sensory language) when they are discussing areas they wish to change or would consider negative emotions or states. You can then test this by asking them to demonstrate the words or actions you have observed to see if it takes them into the negative state they were describing. Another way is to get them to 'act' what they feel and again they will often demonstrate how it is to be anxious or nervous and show you how they need to stand, speak, move etc when in that 'state'.

To replace these negative anchors with positive anchors is called 'collapsing an anchor' and this can also be done by 'chaining anchors'. If the negative anchor is large or strong, chaining anchors is like taking lots of little steps rather than one large leap. These are advanced anchoring skills and only to be practiced as a coach when you have mastered the basics. For now it is important to learn how to set anchors and ensure you or the coachee practices them over and over so that they become very strong and therefore very useful. Choose a 'state' you would like to anchor and use the script from this session to practice it for yourself and then, when you are confident with it, you can use it to assist others. The strongest anchors use all the senses (touch, sound, smell, taste and sound) so ensure you build them all in to get the best results.

Notes page

Personal reflection – Letter of commitment

At the beginning of this program we discussed the value of setting goals and knowing what you want to achieve in life. The letter of commitment exercise is a fabulous exercise to use to help you visualize what life will be like in the future when you have achieved your goals, it's also a great way to motivate you to see what the results will be like. Another good technique for this is to write your letter of commitment to yourself and add lots of personal detail about how proud you will be of yourself when it's all achieved as well as what your life will be like as described in the exercise. When it's complete, rather than put it in your diary, seal it in a self addressed envelope with a stamp and write a date on it which is either 6 or 12 months from now. Then ask a good trusted friend to keep hold of it and pop it into a post box on the date shown on the envelope. To receive your own letter months down the line when you had forgotten all about it is a lovely experience and a great reminder of where you intended to be at that time. As you read through your letter, written in your own handwriting you will discover what a powerful tool this is as you are really self-coaching and making a difference to your life by holding yourself accountable. If you are ahead or on schedule for the areas you wanted to achieve you will feel proud of what you have achieved and if you realize you are behind schedule then it will be a strong reminder of what you committed to do or change in your life and you can consider what you need to do to get back on track to make it happen.

Remember things change and if the goals and desires listed have changed and are no longer what you want then that's fine, nothing is set in stone and you can change them to whatever new things you want. The main point here is that you do something rather than nothing and commit to live the life you desire rather than dream about it.

Session 5

Applying Strategies

"People with clear, written goals,
accomplish far more in a shorter period of time than
people without them could ever imagine." Brian Tracy

Session 5

Applying strategies

Objectives for session 5:

When you've worked through this session, you should be able to:

✓ Put what you've learnt into perspective

✓ Explain the goal setting and summary process to a coachee

✓ Work with someone to practice the coaching session skills

✓ Create a coaching skills documents folder with example scripts and tools

✓ Assess whether you need to repeat any parts of the program

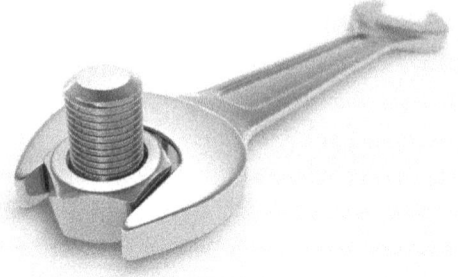

Tools in session 5:

✓ Life areas assessment – for your starting point

✓ Sun diagrams – for ideas of how to achieve goals/issues

✓ Well formed outcome – used to clarify if goals are worth pursuing/achieving as some may have negative outcomes

✓ Goal setting criteria – guidelines of what to cover when setting goals

✓ 5-Step goal setting model – used for goal setting

✓ STEPPPA Model – used for goal setting

✓ TGROW Model – used for goal setting

✓ Skills practise exercises – try out your new skills and techniques

✓ Assessment and evaluation exercise evaluate how much you've learned

Starting points – creating a plan of action

Choosing strategies for self-coaching

Our straightforward five-step process will help you get to the heart of the matter and create specific, effective actions for change:

1. **Areas assessment tools** to decide where to start making changes   *Put plans into action*
2. **Sun diagram** to pinpoint action for improvement
3. **Well formed outcomes** to make sure you're choosing the right goals
4. **Goal setting charts** for strategy and detailed tactics
5. **Summary sheets** for a clear direction and monitoring process

We're going to use the Life Area Assessment document you completed in Session 1 as your starting point and take you through the goal setting process. Remember, you can use any area assessment tool to start the process – for example, the health area assessment we showed you, or one you've created for your situation.

Once you've completed this you'll have the skills to create more goals from other areas you want to focus on and coach others to do the same. You'll have a set process and documents to work from (which you can also tailor to be more specific to your personal or team objectives) and we provide you with all the scripts you may need, too.

Step 1:
Life areas assessment tool

Refer to your document from Session 1.

Choose the areas you want to work on. They could be the ones with the lowest scores, or the area that's the most stressful at the moment.

List the issues/areas for improvement you have identified with those areas and write down goals that will create your desired change.

For example, let's say you want to focus on FINANCES. You might decide that your main issues are that you've got far too much debt. A good goal could be 'I will be debt-free by my birthday'.

Or perhaps you never have enough to splash out at Christmas. A good goal could be 'I will save £1000 to spend on Christmas presents and fun at Christmas!'

> Remember:
>
> Make your goals positive – 'I will buy a new car by Christmas'.
>
> Be clear and specific – rather than say 'I want more money', say 'I'll earn an extra £10,000 a year'.
>
> Choose one specific goal from those you've listed to start with, and work through the following processes.

The next step is the sun diagram which will help you to find out how to achieve the goal i.e. the actions you will need to take.

Step 2:
Create a sun diagram

Create sun diagrams (or mini-mindmaps) for each goal to identify the actions you need to take:

1. Take a piece of plain paper and draw a circle in the middle.

2. Write the name of the goal you've chosen in the circle.

3. Then draw lines from the circle to the outer sides of the paper so it looks a little like a kids drawing of a sun.

4. Brainstorm ideas to make that goal happen.

5. List any and every idea you have.

6. If you fill all the lines add a complete set of new ones all the way around - if your mind sees blank lines it will search the corners to find something to go on them.

Include:

✓ Things that you could do.

✓ People you could ask for help or you could influence.

✓ Any other resources you can think of.

Don't worry if the options don't make sense or you don't know how to do them at this point – just write anything and everything down. All ideas are accepted - you are just brainstorming and can evaluate them later.

Blank sun diagram

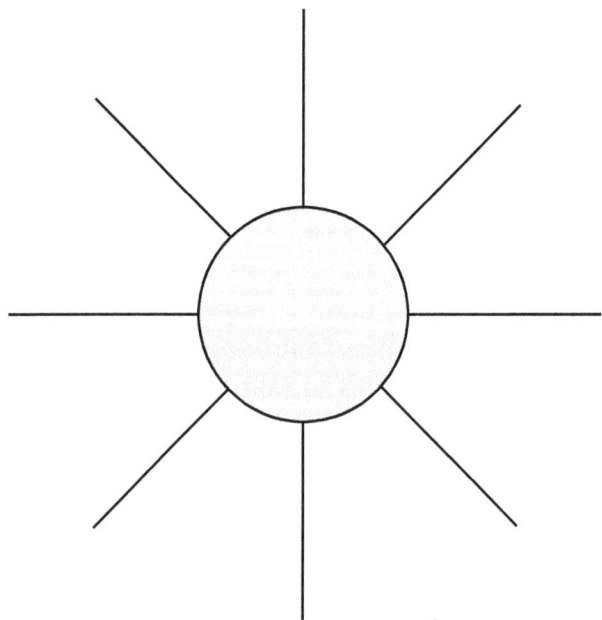

Hint If you need some inspiration, take a look at the example of a filled-in sun diagram in Session 4.

Now look over the sun diagram and select those options you're going to use, that make sense and that you feel you can do. When you've selected lots of options and action-points to achieve your desired goal, you're almost ready to fill out the goal setting process. But before you do, it's important to check that the goal you have chosen is right for you in every way.

Transfer your goal to the well formed outcome process and work through the questions to ensure it is a goal you really want to achieve.

Step 3:
Well formed outcomes

A well formed outcome is a goal that has been questioned, researched and deeply considered, until it is clear and specific.

When you create well formed outcomes, you look at all the possibilities – good and bad, realistic or unrealistic – so you can make the right decisions, and make it easier to achieve your goals.

Use this checklist to make sure your goals are exactly what you want – and to make sure they're clear and realistic.

Here's an example to give you an idea of how it works:

Well formed outcome example:

1. State the goal or desired outcome positively.
   To achieve a grade 5 pay rise.

2. Is it specific or could you define it more, is it measurable?
   Yes.

3. Can you achieve it by yourself?
   Yes, but I would like help from my manager too.

4. Is the goal positive and ethical to benefit you or others around you, i.e. does it have a positive intention?
   Yes, it will benefit me and my family.

5. How will you know when you have it? How will you feel?
   I will feel I have achieved something I worked hard for and be very happy.

6. Why don't you have it now? Has anything stopped you?
   I haven't had enough experience in the past, but feel I am ready now. Perhaps I also needed the confidence to apply.

7. How big a goal is it? Do you need to break it up into smaller goals?
   I need to pass the exam first and then apply for the grading, so 2 smaller goals are required.

8. What are all the steps you need to take?
   Study for my exam in June.
   Pass the exam.
   Speak to my manager and tell her I want to apply for the grading.
   Ask for her help, support and recommendation.
   Apply for the grading.
   Get an interview.
   Pass the interview.
   Get the grading and pay rise.

9. When will you take the first step?
   Today, I will email to register for the exam in June.

10. When will you complete it all?
    I will have completed all the other steps by December.

11. Are there any other ways to get it?
    If I don't pass the exam I can re-sit it in September but if I fail that I will have to wait until June next year. There is no way to get the promotion without passing the exam.

12. What resources do you currently have (physical, emotional, mental, spiritual, financial, knowledge, skills, assistance etc.)?
    I have support from my partner and the time to study, the desire and determination to achieve it.

13. What resources will you need?
    I will need the agreement and support of my line manager.

14. What will you need to give up to have it? How will it affect you (friends, work, relationships, lifestyle etc)?
    I will have to give up my weekends to study which is time with my friends and family, i.e. my social time.

15. What will happen if you don't get it? How will you feel?
If I don't get it I will keep trying until I do, I will feel disappointed.

16. What will happen if you do get it? How will you feel?
I will have better future prospects and more money coming in each month so we can have a holiday away and more treats. I will feel fantastic and proud of myself.

17. If you don't get it, will you lose out on anything?
If I don't get it I will lose out on the money but also feel disappointed. I won't feel that I have achieved my goal and taken control of my life.

18. If you do get it, will you lose out anything?
I won't lose out on anything.

19. What will having it give to you? For what purpose do you want it?
I want it for my achievement, better prospects and more financial security.

20. Will achieving this goal enhance your life and/or others around you?
Yes, mine and my family.

21. Is it a worthwhile goal to aim to achieve? Do you still want to achieve this goal?
Yes, it is worthwhile and I am going to do it.

Exercise: Well formed outcome

Think of a goal you really want to achieve.

Now complete the well formed outcome questions following using the goal you have selected.

Remember you can download a copy of this from the website section on coaching skills (www.UoLearn.com).

Well formed outcome:

1. State the goal or desired outcome positively.

....
....
....

2. Is it specific or could you define it more, is it measurable?

....
....
....

3. Can you achieve it by yourself?

....
....
....

4. Is the goal positive and ethical to benefit you or others around you i.e. does it have a positive intention?

....
....
....

5. How will you know when you have it? How will you feel?

....
....
....

6. Why don't you have it now? Has anything stopped you?

....

....

....

7. How big a goal is it?
   Do you need to break it into smaller goals?

....

....

....

8. What are all the steps you need to take?

....

....

....

9. When will you take the first step?

....

....

....

10. When will you complete it all?

....

....

....

11. Are there any other ways to get it?

....

....

....

12. What resources do you currently have (physical, emotional, mental, spiritual, financial, knowledge, skills, assistance etc.)?

....

....

....

13. What resources will you need?

....

....

....

14. What will you need to give up to have it?
    How will it affect you (friends, work, relationships, lifestyle)?

....

....

....

15. What will happen if you don't get it?
    How will you feel?

....

....

....

16. What will happen if you do get it?
    How will you feel?

....

....

....

17. If you don't get it, will you lose out on anything?

....

....

....

18. If you do get it, will you lose out anything?

....

....

....

19. What will having it give to you?
    For what purpose do you want it?

....

....

....

20. Will achieving this goal enhance your life and/or others
    around you?

....

....

....

21. Is it a worthwhile goal to aim to achieve?
    Do you still want to achieve this goal?

....

....

....

If you're happy with this goal, you can now continue to the goal
setting process.

Step 4:
Goal setting

Choose a goal setting model, either the goal setting chart or one of the other models – STEPPPA or TGROW – and work through your own goal setting exercise. Remember to follow the goal setting criteria.

Goal setting criteria:

✓ Have **target dates** by which you will achieve your goals – be specific with dates.

✓ **Review them daily** – put them in your diary or on your wall and read every day.

✓ Make them **specific**, **detailed and** well defined.

✓ Have a means of **measuring progress** towards achievement – you can assess whether you're achieving or moving towards achieving them, or not.

✓ Choose a **reward or treat** for every goal, to be enjoyed when achieved, this doesn't have to cost money.

✓ Set them **without limits**, no matter how large – dream big, choose anything you want.

✓ **Chunk** into smaller goals if necessary – if it's a large goal, make it into smaller goals which when achieved make up the achievement of the large goal.

✓ Have a **defined support infrastructure** – ask for help, you don't have to do it all by yourself!

Goal setting document:

This is how to make sure you cover all the criteria in the list.

A blank version can be downloaded from the website www.UoLearn.com.

Goal		
Action points		
Why and what benefit		
Who can help and how		
Date to be achieved		
Results and actions so far + / -		
Date actually achieved		
Reward		
Advice for next time		

Using the STEPPPA model:

Subject

What is the subject or issue?

....

....

....

Target

Do you have a clearly defined goal? What is it?

....

....

....

Emotion

Is it important for you to achieve? Are you committed to achieving it? Are you going to take action to achieve it? How motivated are you to achieve it? 0 to 10? (10 = wanting it the most).

....

....

....

Perception

How many ways can you achieve it? How many options do you have? What else could you do?

....

....

....

Plan

Choose one option – what is it?

....

....

....

Pace

When will you achieve it – what are your timescales? Are they realistic? Can you see yourself achieving this?

....

....

....

Adapt or action

Are you ready to put the goal into action or do you need to adapt it? If action – set it in place and monitor it. If adapt – make the changes and work through the steps again.

....

....

....

Using the TGROW model:

Theme

Use the life areas assessment tool to establish the theme or goal.

....

....

....

....

....

Goal - Define one goal.

State the outcome you wish to achieve and by when you intend to achieve it.

Chunk down into smaller goals and timescales if required.

Establish a clear, measurable, specific goal.

....

....

....

....

....

....

....

Reality

Where are you now in relation to this goal?

How great is your concern?

Who else is affected by this issue?

How much control do you have over it?

What action have you taken so far?

What has stopped you going further?

What other resources (skill, time, money, support) do you need?

Where could you acquire them? By when?

....
....
....
....
....
....
....
....
....
....
....
....
....
....

Options

Start to explore the options use sun diagrams if required.

How many different ways could you approach the issue?

List all the alternatives, rule nothing out, no matter how far-fetched it seems.

Which solution seems best to you?

How will this give you the result you seek?

Are there any new options that were not available to you before?

Will

Decide upon the actions required to achieve this goal. Actions should be based on a clear understanding of the issues which also includes timescales/deadlines, a commitment to take action and a way of measuring success.

What course of action will you take and what are the timeframes? Will you agree to select one option?

When will you start work to make it happen?

What is your level of commitment on a scale of zero to ten?

Will you do whatever it takes to get to ten? When?

....

....

....

....

....

....

....

....

....

....

....

....

Once you've worked through your chosen goal setting model, the final stage is to summarize your goals.

If you have a few, it's important to categorize them so that you can see clearly which actions you need to be working on and how well you're achieving your goals. This will also help you to manage time frames and monitor your progress.

If you have only identified one goal at this stage, the summary sheets will help you when you continue to develop your other goals.

Step 5:
Summarize your goals

There are three sheets to use to summarize your goals.

You can download these as word documents from www.UoLearn.com

The sheets are:

➢ Monthly goals: All your goals for the next four weeks.

➢ Twelve month goals:
   What you want to happen in the next year?

➢ Two to five year goals: The longer-term view

Note:

Your short-term monthly goals summaries will be very detailed.

Your twelve-month goals summary, however may well be less so. You know what you want to do over the next year, and more or less when – but the detail might have to come when you do the monthly summary.

Your two-to five-year goals summary will certainly be less detailed. You might not have specific dates for some of these goals as they could be a while away or change over time. Some could also be 'wish' goals that you'd like to list but you might be unsure of how to achieve them right now. Still list them, though, as you'll work out the 'how' as you go along!

Summarizing overview:

With your summaries to hand and up-to-date:

✓ You'll know **exactly** what you need to do over the coming month.

✓ You'll have a **timetable** of what you're going to achieve over the coming year.

✓ You'll have a good **outline** of what you want to achieve in the future.

You don't need to write the whole goal as you've written it on your goal setting sheets. You can just summarize it – just as long as you recognize what the goal is. If you need to clarify some action points or remind yourself of the detail you can go back to your goal setting sheets, sun diagrams or well formed outcomes at any time.

The summarizing process:

Look through the dates you've identified for each goal and categorize them in order.

Add them to each relevant sheet.

You can also split each goal-summary sheet into sections, such as:

Financial goals

Health goals

General goals

Personal goals

Family goals

Work goals

Traveling goals

Study goals

Spiritual goals

Relationship goals

Basically, use any sections you want that are relevant or mean something to you.

> **Tips:**
>
> Place all your goal setting documents in a ring binder so you can refer to them quickly and easily whenever you wish – you'll then have a Goals Folder.
>
> Set aside a time towards the end of each month to prepare your detailed Goal Summary for the next month and to re-assess your longer-term goal summaries.

Here's an example of how someone chose to do theirs. Your goals summaries will probably look completely different. You might have lots more goals and use different categories. This is just to give you an idea. Blank goal forms can be downloaded from www.UoLearn.com

1 Month goal setting summary example

Yours may be different categories and a lot more goals, this is to give you an idea.

Current date: 1st January

Goal end date: 31st January

Category: Finance goals

Business

Secure the Tailor contract to receive £5000 revenue - Jan 15th

Ask personnel about the tax reduction in my wage last month – Jan 10th

Personal

Cash in the ISA to pay the credit card – Jan 29th

Save £50 per month in the new account – Jan 5th

Start a new ISA - Jan 31st

Pay the car insurance, set up a direct debit – Jan 16th

Category Health goals

Get back to the gym on Monday and Thursdays – Jan 3rd and weekly

Ask Debbie to run with me on Saturday mornings – Jan 5th and weekly

Reduce caffeine and alcohol to 1 cup a day – Jan 10th and ongoing

Enquire about a detox course at the gym, ring reception – Jan 4th

Book in for a massage – Jan 20th

Category Work goals

Speak to manager about the promotion and whether to apply – Jan 4th

Book on new study course - Jan 4th

Sort out flexi time and allocate holidays for next 6 months – Jan 10th

Call team meeting to assess progress with Brook case – Jan 6th

12 months goal setting summary example

Yours may be different categories and a lot more goals, this is to give you an idea.

Start date: 1st January

Goal end date: 31st December

Category study goals

Sign onto the accountancy course – Feb 3rd

Complete the accountancy course – May 30th

Buy books for course – Feb 10th

Category family goals

Book holiday for July– May 5th

Visit Uncle Ross with the kids – Mar 7th- Mar 10th

Book baby sitter for Feb 5th – Feb 3rd

Ice skating with kids – Feb 23rd

Help David start high school – Sept 3rd

Category relationship goals

Have a date night alone with my wife once per month starting – Feb 5th

Book weekend away for Valentine's night – Feb 4th

Category general goals

Redecorate living room on week off Sep 1st – Sept 10th

Gardeners in Oct 20th for 2 weeks

Buy new sofa in time for Xmas next year - Nov

Buy Xmas presents early and be organized! Start shopping Oct

Fund raise for Dec 5k marathon – start Oct

Train for marathon all year – start March

---

2 to 5 years goal setting summary example

You may not have specific dates for some of these goals as they could be a while away or change, some of these could also be 'wish' goals that you would like to list as you may be unsure of how to achieve them right now, still list them as you will work out how as you go along!

Start date: 1st January 20XX

Goal end date: 31st December 20XX

Category general

Pay off the mortgage in 5 years

Go to Africa for my wedding anniversary in 3 years

Save £5000 pounds for the trip

Go to Andrew's graduation

Do a charity bungee jump

Move to a smaller house with a large garden

Buy a motorbike and learn to ride

Dig out the camping stuff from the loft and go on a camping trip in France

---

Use the documents provided and tailor them so they're personal to you.

You may wish to re-create the sheets so you can stick them on your wall or put them in your diary, anywhere you will be able to view them each day. Especially the 1 month goal setting summary which is your guide for the month.

Goal setting tips:

As you move along you might decide to scrap some goals and strike them out. You might add some or change them.

Any that you don't achieve in the month that you still wish to achieve can be transferred over to the next month.

Make sure you update these sheets each month and stay on top of your goal setting.

Skills to practice

Practice the skills learned from this program as often as you can. Ensure whoever you work with understands you are learning and gives their permission to work with you. And stay within your boundaries and competencies. Once you feel you're able to use these skills and strategies successfully for yourself, you'll be able to start to apply them to a full coaching session.

Full coaching session

When you're ready to practice a whole coaching session, the following exercise will help you and your partner or volunteer coachee. Ask them for feedback to help you improve your skills.

Exercise: Coaching with the five-step process

Volunteer coachee: Use a real issue you want to work on.

Coach: You're starting from the first session, so you need to build rapport and discuss the ground rules of the session for both parties. If you choose to create your own written agreement to cover rules and boundaries, do this first. You might need several sessions to complete the whole process.

Use any of the strategies and documents you've been introduced to during this program. Feel free to adapt them for more specific use.

Follow the Five-Stage program for effective goal setting and making changes.

Coachee

✓ Select a goal or issue that you'd really like help with – one that you're prepared to share in detail with the coach.

✓ You're responsible for providing feedback to the coach, so you'll need to consider all the core coaching skills and strategies the coach uses and how effective they were in their role.

Coach

Remember to be aware of and use any of the skills and tools you've covered. (You won't need all of these – select the ones you feel the most comfortable with, but you must always use the core skills)

Follow the core coaching dos and don'ts

✓ Maintain and discuss the boundaries for confidentiality

✓ Demonstrate active listening and use good questioning skills

✓ Be respectful and honest

✓ Be non-judgmental

✓ Empathize

✓ Build and maintain rapport

✓ Observe your own and their body language

✓ Summarize

✓ Give constructive positive feedback

✓ Challenge and question appropriately

✗ Don't discuss yourself

✗ Don't lose track of time

✗ Don't end the session abruptly

✗ Don't take phone calls or allow the session to be interrupted

Use the three W's to structure the session:

✓ Where are you now?

✓ What do you want/where do you want to be?

✓ What are you going to do about it?

**Work with issues/fears around change
and the comfort zone**

Listen carefully and observe your coachee:

✓ How do they present themselves?
  Are they aggressive, submissive or assertive?

✓ How could they enhance their own communication skills?

✓ What is their learning style? Use the questionnaire if you wish
  – adapt your coaching style and use of language to suit their
  dominant style

✓ What are their other styles, such as visual, auditory or
  kinesthetic?

✓ Where do they fit with the I'm OK – You're OK model?

✓ Look out for hidden issues and refer for appropriate help
  from a professional coach or therapist if required.

Use the perceptual positions to gently challenge and help
to reframe their views if negative, using positive language and
feedback to motivate

Use any of the following tools for effective change:

- ✓ Life areas assessment for a good starting point
- ✓ New behavior generator
- ✓ Anchors and pattern breaks/interrupts
- ✓ Confidence-building techniques: positive beliefs exercises, letter of commitment, letter of positivity
- ✓ Relaxation technique for calm and focus
- ✓ Chunking for breaking down large goals or obtaining more/less information
- ✓ Sun diagrams
- ✓ Well formed outcomes
- ✓ Goal setting models
- ✓ Summary goal sheets

Assessment and evaluation

Complete the following quiz to assess how much of the program you're familiar with. Remember you're able to use and repeat this program as many times as you wish. You'll also need to practice with volunteers as often as possible to enhance your skills and make them as natural as possible.

Full answers and a version with space for the answers are on the website (www.UoLearn.com). The number in brackets is the total number of answers for that question.

1. What are the three perceptual positions? (3)

2. What is a 'mind read'? (1)

3. What does NLP stand for? (1)

4. What's the difference between coaching and therapy? (1)

5. List three types of coaching. (3)

6. What does 'Conscious Competence' mean? (1)

7. List four types of learning styles. (4)

8. When would a coachee need to be referred to an external professional? (1)

9. List five words used to start open questions. (5)

10. Which word do you avoid using when coaching? (1)

11. List three things you can do to create rapport. (3)

12. What is the best way to give feedback? (1)

13. Do you sit facing a coachee or to the side on an angle?　(1)

14. List three ways you could break a coachee's pattern.　(3)

15. Is 'fruit' a chunk up or down from 'apple'?　(1)

16. Would you chunk up or down to get more detailed information from a coachee?　(1)

17. How would you get a coachee to consider their impact on others?　(1)

18. List five ground rules of effective coaching.　(5)

19. What is a limiting belief?　(1)

20. What does a sun diagram highlight?　(1)

21. What are three different preferred senses/learning/communication methods?　(3)

22. What are the five senses anchors can be based on?　(5)

23. What (typically) would someone be doing when they look up to the right when answering a question?　(1)

24. What would you use The Three W's for?　(1)

25. What are the four 'I'm OK–You're OK' models of behavior?　(4)

26. Why use a well formed outcome?　(1)

27. What is generally the biggest fear people have of being out of their comfort zone?　(1)

28. What is the percentage split for physiology, voice and words when people are not communicating effectively?　(3)

29. What would you do if you were to micro-mirror someone?　(1)

30. What does psychogeography mean?　(1)

Total　**(60)**

Farewell and thank you!

We really hope you've enjoyed working through this program with us, and that you've acquired many skills and tools to help you coach yourself and others.

Remember, you now have coaching skills but are not a qualified coach. Please be mindful of that when working with others and refer for specialist help if appropriate.

Having a clear direction and then setting your goals really works. If you can make goal setting and reviewing your direction and progress a regular part of your life, you'll be far more likely to achieve all that you desire.

In the 1950s, students at Yale University were surveyed and asked whether they had written goals. Only three per cent had.

When they were questioned again, 20 years later, it was found that the three per cent were worth more than the other 97 per cent combined. They also had better health and better personal relationships.

An unwritten goal is a dream.

Goal setting works.

So, finally ...

- ✓ Pick the strategies, solutions and resources that suit you best
- ✓ Apply them consistently
- ✓ Practice
- ✓ Believe that you can achieve anything you wish
- ✓ Remember, this is your choice and your life

We've given you signposts, ideas and, hopefully, inspiration - only you can make the difference.

So now it's over to you!

A bee defies science as it shouldn't be able to fly. Aerodynamically, bees shouldn't be able to fly because their body is so much larger than their wing span. Yet no one seems to have told the bee it can't fly so it does fly. In fact, it can also fly backwards, and there's only one aeroplane in the world that's capable of that!

What have you been told or believe that you can't do that you could be doing?

What if you just decide that you can do anything you want to and ignore everyone else and make like a bee?

- ✓ **Bee free!**
- ✓ **Bee yourself!**
- ✓ **Bee happy!**

Good luck in the future!

'Why follow the path when you can create your own trail?'

Kathryn Critchley

If you've enjoyed this program, you'll find the list of our other programs at our website: www.UoLearn.com.
Remember you can find a printable workbook with all the exercises and downloadable blank templates from the book at the same site.

Further reading

"The things I want to know are in books; my best friend is
the man who'll get me a book I ain't read."
Abraham Lincoln

Further reading

General:

Words That Change Minds: Mastering The Language And Influence, Shelly Rose Charvet, Kendall Hunt (1997)

Influence: The Psychology Of Persuasion, Robert B Cialdini, Collins (1998)

Increase your Influence, A guide to developing the 7 traits of influential people, Lois Burton and Deborah Dalley, Universe of Learning (2009)

Seven Habits Of Highly Effective People, Stephen R Covey, Simon and Schuster (1999)

Thinking Styles : Relationship Strategies That Work, Fiona Beddoes-Jones, BJA Associates (1999)

Lateral Thinking, Edward De Bono, Penguin

Thinking Course, Edward De Bono, Petanco (1989)

Strategies Of Genius, Robert Dilts, Meta Publications (1996)

Emotional Intelligence, Daniel P Goleman, Bantam, (2005)

Believe You Can, Clive Gott, (2004)

Excuse Me Your Life Is Waiting, Lynn Grabhorn, Hodder and Staughton (2004)

Mind Over Mood: Change How You Feel By Changing The Way You Think, Dennis Greenberger and Christine A Padessky, The Guilford Press (1995)

Turtles All The Way Down, John Grinder and Judith DeLozier, Metamorphous Press (1996)

I'm OK You're OK, Thomas A Harris, Arrow (1995)

Think And Grow Rich, Napoleon Hill, Vermilon (2004)

Counseling Skills and Theory,
Margaret Hough, Hodder and Staughton (2003)
Teaching With the Brain in Mind, Eric Jensen, Association for
Supervision and Curriculum Development (1998)
Notes From A Friend,
Anthony Robbins, Simon and Schuster (1996)
Power To Influence, Anthony Robbins, CD Set
The 11th Element, Robert Scheinfeld, Wiley (2003)
Understanding Misunderstandings,
Nancy Slessenger, Vine House (2003)
Permission To Succeed,
Noah St John, Health Communications (1999)
**Creative Training Techniques Handbook: Tips, Tactics, and
How- To's for Delivering Effective Training,** Robert Pike,
Lakewood Publications (1994)
**Experiential Learning: Experience as the Source of Learning
and Development,** David A Kolb, Prentice-Hall (1984)

Coaching & NLP:

The Structure Of Magic, Richard Bandler and John Grinder, Science and Behavior Books (1975)

The NLP Coach, Ian McDermot and Wendy Jago, Piatkus (2001)

Coaching: Evoking Excellence in Others,
James Flaherty, Butterworth-Heinemann Ltd (2004)

The Inner Game of Work,
Timothy Gallwey, Random House Trade Paperbacks (2001)

Sourcebook of Magic, L Michael Hall, Barbara P Belnap and Barbara Belnap, The Crown House Publishing (2001)

Be Your Own Life Coach: How to Take Control of Your Life and Achieve Your Wildest Dreams,
Fiona Harrold, Coronet Books (2001)

Coaching for Commitment,
Dennis C Kinlaw, Jossey-Bass/Pfeiffer (1999)

NLP at Work: The Difference that Makes a Difference in Business, Sue Knight, 2nd Edition, Nicholas Brealey Pub. (2002)

The really good fun cartoon book of NLP,
Philip Miller, Crown, (2008)

Coaching and Mentoring, Nigel MacLennan, Gower (1995)

The Life Coaching Handbook: Everything You Need to Be an Effective Life Coach, Curly Martin, Crown House (2001)

Performance Coaching: The Handbook for Managers, HR Professionals and Coaches,
Angus McLeod, Crown House Publishing (2003)

Coaching for Performance: Growing People, Performance and Purpose, John Whitmore, Nicholas Brealey Publishing (2002)

Index

"But words are things, and a small drop of ink,
Falling like dew, upon a thought, produces
That which makes thousands, perhaps millions, think."
Lord Byron

Index

Universe of Learning books

"Books are the quietest and most constant of friends; they are the most accessible and wisest of counsellors, and the most patient of teachers." Charles W. Eliot

About the publishers

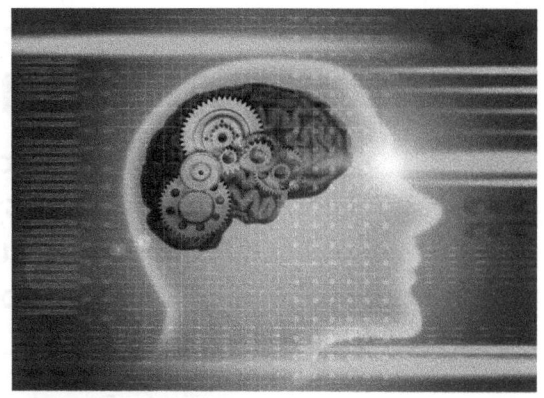

Universe of Learning Limited is a small publisher based in the UK with production in England and America. Our authors are all experienced trainers or teachers who have taught their skills for many years. We are actively seeking qualified authors and if you visit the authors' section on www.UoLearn.com you can find out how to apply.

If you would like any of our current authors (including Kathryn Critchley) to speak at your event please do visit their own websites (for Kathryn it's www.realifeltd.co.uk) or email them through the author section of the UoLearn site.

If you would like to purchase larger numbers of books then please do contact us (sales@UoLearn.com). We give discounts from 5 books upwards. For larger volumes we can also quote for changes to the cover to accommodate your company logo and to the interior to brand it for your company.

We have two main imprints – the Skills Training Course (like this book) where the books are illustrated with photographs and the Easy 4 me 2 Learn range where the illustrations are fun cartoons. For either imprint the aim is to take people through the development of skills by a range of exercises.

If you have any feedback about this book or other topics that you'd like to see us cover please do contact us at support@UoLearn.com.

Keep Learning!

Stress Management Skills Training Course

Exercises and techniques to identify the symptoms of stress and anxiety Build success in your life by goal setting, relaxation and changing thinking with NLP

ISBN: 978-1-84937-002-8, from www.UoLearn.com

✓ Free downloadable workbook
✓ Stress audit questionnaire
✓ Exercises to help you throughout the book
✓ Realistic methods to help you change the way you think about situations
✓ Techniques for relaxation
✓ Easy 4 step goal setting process

Developing Your Influencing Skills,

How to influence people by increasing your credibility, trustworthiness and communication skills

ISBN: 978-1-84937-022-6, Order at www.UoLearn.com

What are the characteristics that make some people more influential than others?

This book will give you the keys to successfully increase your influence at work and at home.
In this book you will discover how to:
✓ Decide what your influencing goals are and state them in a compelling way
✓ Find ways to increase your credibility rating
✓ Develop stronger and more trusting relationships
✓ Inspire others to follow your lead
✓ Become a more influential communicator

This book is packed with case studies, exercises and practical tips to help develop the traits required to become more influential.

Speed Writing
Skills Training Course

Speedwriting for faster note taking and dictation, an alternative to shorthand to help you take notes.

ISBN 978-1-84937-011-0, from www.UoLearn.com

✓ "The principles are very easy to follow, and I am already using it to take notes."
✓ "BakerWrite is the easiest shorthand system I have come across."
✓ "I will use this system all the time."
✓ "Your system is so easy to learn and use."

Study Skills Training Course

How to pass your exam, test or coursework easily

Improve your learning skills to pass exams and assessments, take notes, memorize facts and speed read, for studying at school and college
Free downloadable workbook

ISBN: 978-1-84937-005-9, Order at www.UoLearn.com

Study should be about extracting the information you need from the sources available as easily and quickly as possible. This book has a series of easy to follow exercises to help you become a super-learner.

Dr Greenhall's techniques helped her to get a first class honors degree in physics and chemistry, a doctorate in science and an MA in education, easily and with little effort. Guided exercises will help you to learn the secrets of these successes.

"Don't wait until everything is just right.
It will never be perfect.
There will always be challenges, obstacles
and less than perfect conditions.
So what.
Get started now.
With each step you take, you will
grow stronger and stronger,
more and more skilled,
more and more self-confident
and more and more successful."

Mark Victor Hansen

Lightning Source UK Ltd.
Milton Keynes UK
UKHW052157021218
333358UK00011B/363/P